Are there times when your emotions are so out of control that you think you're losing your sanity? Is there a correlation between your mood swings and your hormones? When Jean Lush addressed the subject of hormonal activity and women's emotions on James Dobson's "Focus on the Family" radio broadcast, the show received the largest response ever. In *Emotional Phases of a Woman's Life*, Jean Lush and Patricia H. Rushford trace the hormonal changes through a woman's life and the emotional states that may accompany them.

The straightforward counsel in this book will enable you to approach each of life's changes (PMS, postpartum blues, mid-life malaise, perimenopause, and menopause) with a positive outlook. You'll gain an understanding of your special emotional needs and learn the value of offering support to other women. Best of all, you'll be assured that you're *normal*.

For every woman who needs to know that her emotional swings are not "all in her head," here is an excellent resource. It's also a great book to help husbands, pastors, and counselors understand women better.

By Jean Lush with Pamela Vredevelt
Mothers and Sons

By Patricia H. Rushford
What Kids Need Most in a Mom
The Help, Hope, & Cope Book for
    People With Aging Parents
Have You Hugged Your Teenager Today?
Caring for Your Sick Child
Kristen's Choice
Love Is a Many Splintered Thing

Emotional Phases of a Woman's Life

JEAN LUSH

with Patricia H. Rushford

Fleming H. Revell Company
Old Tappan, New Jersey

The Library of Congress has cataloged the first printing of this book as follows:

Lush, Jean.
    Emotional phases of a woman's life.

    1. Endocrine gynecology—Popular works.   2. Women—Psychology.   3. Emotions   I. Rushford, Patricia H.
    II. Title.
RG159.L87   1986   155.6'33   86-33931
ISBN 0-8007-5377-1

Copyright © 1987 by Jean Lush and Patricia H. Rushford
Published by the Fleming H. Revell Company
Old Tappan, New Jersey 07675
Printed in the United States of America

TO Lyall . . .
and the rest of the family
for their understanding
and "pressure" to get the job done

——————————————— ટ⸱

Acknowledgments

A special thank you to:
Dr. James Dobson and the staff of Focus on the Family and Fritz Ridenour for their support and encouragement in getting started.

Dr. David Lush and his wife, Gail, Dr. Grady Hughes and his wife, Heather, Dr. Kirk Farnsworth and all the staff of Crista Counseling Services, Dr. Ronald Margolis, Dr. Frank Crealock, and Dr. Hal Zimmer, Dr. Joe Roncskevitz, Sheila Miller, RN, Beck Lee, RN, Margo Power, RN, Dixie Mace, Sue Mobley, and the Reverend Brad Gil and his wife, Beth, Lois Williams, and Ruby MacDonald for their critique, encouragement, support, and professional expertise.

Adele Johnson, Gay Somero, Tony Glazier, Jan Harper and all the women who wrote and called and gave me valuable insight into the emotional and hormonal problems women suffer.

The women's ministries of Woodenville Alliance Church and the Sisters Club for their encouragement, prayers and continual support.

Contents

Part II: The Romantic Phase ——————— 59

Part III: Mid-Life Malaise ——————— 109

Part V: Postmenopause ————————— 205

Introduction ──────── ৡ৶

Annette, a 35-year-old woman, phoned me after a recent radio broadcast of Dr. James Dobson's program, "Focus on the Family."

"Oh, Jean," she said, "I heard you on the air this morning and thought maybe you could help me. Your description of a premenopausal woman fits me like a tailor-made suit. One day I feel great—like I can deal with any crisis—the next I'm in total despair. I've had thoughts of leaving my family and even considered how the world would be better off without me. When I heard you this morning I thought maybe you would understand. Do you?"

"Yes," I answered, "I do, and I don't think you're going crazy. Your body is simply sending messages to your mind that make you think you're going crazy."

"Oh," she said. "You mean my body is telling my mind that I'm crazy, but I'm really not?"

"Something like that, yes," I replied.

"Oh, thank goodness," she sighed. "I can live with that."

Phone calls and letters like Annette's have been pouring into my home since I first appeared on Dr. Dobson's program several years ago. For many women like Annette, simply knowing the source of the problem helps them cope. Of course, knowing isn't going to bring about a cure, but it is a start.

In *Emotional Phases of a Woman's Life* we'll be exploring emotions such as mood swings, depression, and low self-esteem to learn how they relate to the hormonal activity going on within our bodies.

With all the information that has been distributed over the last few years through books, women's magazines, and television, I thought women could easily find the answers they needed. Yet the truth about hormonal imbalances in women and how they affect a woman's physical, psychological, social, and emotional life is still shrouded in a dark gray cloud.

In 1983 Niels H. Lauersen, M.D., and Eileen Stukane wrote a book titled *Premenstrual Syndrome and You*. These words appeared on the cover:

> Over 5 million women are in the dark about a severe hormonal imbalance affecting them 10 days out of every month. They are frightened by violent fluctuations in mood, depression, and weight gain, and they don't know what's causing them. It is one of the greatest medical and political controversies of our time. . . .[1]

Premenstrual Syndrome and You was written to clear up controversies—to lift the fog. Now practically everyone knows about PMS and many other hormonally caused problems, but many questions still remain unanswered.

Is it any wonder? Doctors themselves can't seem to agree. In light of all the evidence, some doctors pat women on the head and say, "It's just female nerves," hand them a prescription for an antidepressant, or send them to a family therapist.

Some of the concerns and questions doctors raise are valid; some are not. Here are just a few:

- Are these symptoms psychosomatic?
- Don't hormone treatments increase the risk of cancer?
- Haven't women always been irrational and unstable creatures?
- The symptoms are too many and too varied.
- The illness and treatment haven't been scientifically proven.

The millions of us who have experienced hormonal changes and know the effect they have on us find it ridiculous that many professional, intelligent people deny such problems exist. But they do.

Just the other day I heard a newscaster report on the American Psychiatric Association's lobby to label premenstrual syndrome as a psychological disorder rather than a physical problem. Why? For one thing, there is fear that chauvinistic men will use the fact that hormones affect us as a tool to keep us from attaining high-level positions.

Poppycock! The very fact that we women cope with drastic monthly changes within our bodies should prove us quite capable of handling anything. Look at Queen Victoria. According to diaries kept during her reign, she suffered terribly with premenstrual syndrome, yet this popular monarch ruled England for sixty years.

My goal in writing this book is to provide clear answers for those women who may be confused, frustrated, misunderstood, mistreated, or untreated. I also want to provide hope and help to those who feel victimized by their hormones or the medical profession.

In this book we'll explore the various phases of a woman's life, examining the hormonal changes that at times seem to govern her body and mind. As we approach each phase, we'll examine changes that may be taking place and offer helpful advice for overcoming the problem areas.

Few women can live a lifetime without experiencing some discomfort due to hormonal changes. Many women, especially those with severe symptoms, may feel victimized by the changes taking place in their bodies and their minds. But there is hope, and there are answers.

There are times when it is important to allow yourself to know what you are feeling and simply accept it as reality. Feeling bad or guilty, on the other hand, starts a judgment process that can end in suppressing those very feelings that it is important to recognize. I can understand that many Christian women might be afraid of acknowledging such feelings for fear that it might lead to acting on them. One of women's greatest assets and greatest strengths, however, is that they generally do know how to separate their feelings from their actions. During times of changing hormonal levels a woman may *feel* vicious and witchy, but she usually carries out her required duties amazingly well.

I've spent over thirty years counseling women and their families. In that time I have seen slow but steady growth in understanding women and the emotional problems that can arise as a result of hormonal imbalances. I'm grateful for the progress that has been made, but we've a long way to go.

My sincerest desire is that *Emotional Phases of a Woman's Life* will shed a clearer light to brighten your path as you walk through the emotional and hormonal phases of your life.

Emotional Phases of a Woman's Life

Part I

Entering Womanhood

Moving through the emotional phases of life is a lot like traveling cross-country in a jumbo jet. Some women experience little turbulence, while others feel their plane is hitting every air pocket, thunderstorm, and lightning bolt in the sky.

The first leg of our flight begins with the earliest emotional phase of a woman's life, as she enters into womanhood. There are a lot of advantages and a few disadvantages to being a female, and we'll be talking about a few of them in chapter one.

In chapter two we will focus on a woman experiencing the emotional side of her menses. Chapter three will give us a review of the female reproductive system and how it works.

There are times when our reproductive system is not only a bit of a drag, but a real pain. In chapter four I'll be talking about dysmenorrhea (painful periods). Chapter five will offer help in overcoming the emotional and physical discomforts of the menstrual cycle.

On Being
a Woman   ෨

Have you ever complained about God's "unfairness" in letting you suffer through some of the emotional and hormonal storms raging through your body?

A woman at a recent conference did. "Jean," she said, "tell us how we can overcome the curse of premenstrual tension."

"Look," I said, "I don't think of it as a curse. We're talking about a wonderful reproductive system here. Our reproductive system can make us mothers. It gives us the capacity to love. Like roses, we must live with a few thorns and learn to appreciate the overall beauty of being a woman."

Many women in our productive and busy society have developed a negative attitude toward the menses, menopause, and other hormone-related changes that may cause discomfort. I suppose it's only natural. At times being a woman can be a downright nuisance. In fact, some of the negative feelings we have about it arise from the chemical or hormonal changes going on inside our bodies.

I would like us, however, to approach the emotional and hormonal phases of our lives with as much of a positive attitude as we can muster. The apostle Paul entreats us to dwell on "whatever is true, whatever is honorable, whatever is just, whatever is pure, whatever is lovely, whatever is gracious, if there is any excellence, if there is anything worthy of praise, think about these things" (Philippians 4:8 RSV).

By using this Bible verse, I don't mean to give the impression that living on a diet of high hopes and positive thoughts can eliminate all troubles. That's not realistic at all. But we would do well to take Paul's advice. Let's pause and appreciate the roses: the lovely, intricately made women that we are.

What Makes a Woman a Woman and Not a Man?

As I think about the unique differences between men and women, I'm reminded of a story I heard on Doctor Dobson's program a while back.

In the late sixties two long-haired hippies were involved in a minor motorcycle accident. One was a male and the other a female. They were taken to the emergency room of a local hospital and were waiting to be treated.

A nurse came in to assess their injuries. Because they looked alike, she was uncertain as to which was the man and which was the woman, so she decided to ask a question that would determine the answer.

She said, quite casually, "Which one of you has a menstrual cycle?"

The short one with the deep voice looked out from under his mane and said, "Not me, man. I got da Honda."

We are different anatomically, hormonally, socially, sexually, psychologically, and emotionally. God created men and women as two distinct pieces of a puzzle. When the right two pieces come together, what a sizzling, fascinating, and exciting picture we make.

Within us is a mechanism by which human life is propagated. In our wombs a seed is fertilized and planted. A baby develops and grows, nourished by our own blood. We can gaze down at the face of a purplish, homely newborn baby and call him adorable.

But it's more than having babies. Women have certain qualities that make us nurturers, encouragers, and lovers. We are strong, able to endure great hardships, suffering, and pain. We are by nature romantic, beguiling, and sensuous. And men love us.

We have many reasons to enjoy our roles as women. So, simply consider what is true, honorable, pure, lovely, gracious, and excellent in being a woman, and dwell on that.

Feeling Good About Being You

Low self-esteem is one of the most common problems among women. There are many factors that go into the development of self-esteem. Much depends on the way we were brought up—our childhood traumas and conditioning—and on the way we view life.

I often talk with women who suffer from overwhelming guilt and a sense of failure due to hormonal problems that affect their emotional health.

One young woman, Margaret, who suffers from premenstrual syndrome, explained it this way:

> I try so hard to live an upstanding Christian life, but the days just before my period, I lose it all. I feel like I'm standing outside my body watching this horrid person that looks like me scream, cry, and throw temper tantrums. I try to stop, but I can't. I hate myself for it. When I went to my

pastor, he suggested I might be possessed by a demon. My psychiatrist thought a few weeks in the mental ward, along with a tranquilizer or antidepressant, might help. How can I be a Christian and still act like I do? It doesn't make sense.

I know just what Margaret means. I, too, suffered from premenstrual syndrome. It was so bad at times I was afraid my behavior would completely destroy my ministry. My self-esteem dropped to an all-time low. I felt there was something terribly wrong with me. Other women seemed so pious and in control; then there was me.

"Then There Was Me"

I was raised in Australia by very British, very proper parents. In my growing-up years I developed extremely low self-esteem. I came from a superintellectual family, and was late in maturing. I never felt clever enough for my family. I always felt I couldn't live up to what I *thought* my mother wanted of me. I knew I'd never be as ladylike as my mother, or as beautiful.

When I reached the age of sixteen, Mother decided it was time for me to be "proper." She especially concerned herself with pounding and molding me into an acceptable British lady.

In my case that wasn't easy. It was jolly hard for her to get me to wear the corsets, pearls, and gloves that young ladies of the day were required to don for every occasion.

One of the integral requirements of Victorian propriety was absolute control of one's feelings: A lady did not show her emotions. After years of conditioning, my mother finally succeeded in making me suitably stoic.

Don't misunderstand me; I loved my mother dearly. She only brought me up the way she had been trained by her mother. But, because of this conditioning, I grew up to be a

woman who was very uncomfortable about expressing how
I felt.

On top of my British training, even more restraint
seemed required of me when I became a Christian. I
thought that as a Christian I was not allowed to feel the negative emotions that almost overwhelmed me on those days
before my period.

That was another thing: One never talked about *that*. If
you *had* to discuss it, you would whisper, "I'm coming on
unwell." Many proper ladies simply went to bed, leaving
their work for the maids.

When I first "came on unwell," my mother briefly told
me what to do, then said, "You will never discuss being unwell with your friends." Then she added sternly, "Only
very low-class girls do that."

I grew up thinking it was all right to swoon or to have a
bad head, but never, never, never were we to discuss our
bodies or what was happening to them. I remember one day
mentioning the word *brassiere*, to my father. Let me tell you,
Mother went white. She rolled her eyes and gave me that
tight-lipped look, as only Mother could. Later she told me,
"You shamed me in front of your father." She proceeded to
let me know that in all the years they'd been married (she'd
had four children), Father had never even seen a nappy
(British for diaper). And I, rebellious child that I was, had to
go and talk about a bra.

I eventually got married, and to my utter shock a few
months after our wedding, my very understanding husband
said to me, "I'm not going to listen to you today." (We were
having an argument about money or some such thing.)
"We'll talk about it after your period, when you're back to
your old self."

I couldn't believe that he would mention *it*, but I was
thankful. I'd never really related my days of being an abso-

lute monster to my "coming on unwell." After that I pretty much isolated myself during those days.

A Thorn in the Flesh

My husband and I, with our three children, eventually came to America to work in a full-time Christian ministry. I was horrified to think that someone would uncover my terrible dark secret. How could I ever manage to live a life of service to God when, for three or four days out of the month, I turned into a monster?

Eventually I learned that I was not a freak of nature, as I had suspected. For years I had thought I was somehow different, perhaps even crazy. I'd look around at other women, and they would seem to have themselves all together. With my up and down moods, I felt completely unfit for Christian service, but I couldn't tell anyone. Proper Christians didn't talk about it, either. I felt ashamed and guilt-ridden over my hateful thoughts and angry, destructive words.

Finally, I decided to go to the Lord in prayer and seek healing for this strange malady with which I'd been afflicted. I had the job of supervising a dorm full of girls and simply couldn't let them see their adviser and role model literally fall apart once a month. I was certain God would heal me so I could look good to them.

I took my Bible and went out into the prayer garden under the trees. I planned on staying there until I'd been completely healed, no matter how long it took. I prayed and prayed and felt that I really must have been healed. The next time I was unwell, I'd have none of the horrid symptoms that had plagued me and my poor family in the past.

Well, the next period was better. I had the physical problems, with cramping, backaches, and dragginess, but the bitter emotions were gone. The next month came along, and

I wasn't worried a bit. I knew I'd sail through my cycle with a breeze at my back.

Well, the breeze turned into a savage wind—the symptoms returned. I went back out to the prayer garden to have another talk with God. During prayer, the well-being I'd felt the month before returned, and again I thought I had been healed.

The third month came along, and my premenstrual malady hit even worse than before. "What's going on here?" I asked God. I went back to the garden, remembering something about doing it three times. Every time I'd gone out, the Lord had led me to read different Bible passages. This particular day, God showed me a passage I didn't want to see: 2 Corinthians 12:7–10.

In that text, Paul asked God to remove his problem, his thorn in the flesh, three times. God did not. "Each time He said, 'No. But I am with you; that is all you need. My power shows up best in weak people'" (2 Corinthians 12:9 TLB).

I knew in that moment I would not be totally healed of premenstrual syndrome. But I also knew that healing would take place continuously and that by spending time with the Lord and leaning on Him, especially during the days when my symptoms were most severe, I would make it through.

In fact, my premenstrual days became a time of spiritual refreshment for me. Had I been totally healed, I might have sailed through life being cocky enough to think I could make it on my own. And today, instead of being able to tell women that I understand, I might be one of those unsympathetic people who say, "Come on, buck up. After all, it's only in your mind."

I thank God now that I did not have an easy time of it. Instead I felt strongly motivated to find answers for myself and for other women like me who struggle with possible hormone imbalances.

Postpartum blues, premenstrual tension, and other hor-monally related problems can cause havoc with our minds as well as our bodies. They can become a despised thorn in the flesh that we long to yank out. But thorns don't always come out.

Women have been and always will be a mystery to hu-mankind. Men can never know what it is like to ovulate, to menstruate, to give birth, and to go through menopause.

Women are different from men—uniquely so—and we can feel good and wonderful and positive about our bodies and ourselves.

2

The Emotional Side of Menses _____ ॐ

In chapter one we briefly covered the effect our emotions and hormone imbalances have on our attitudes and self-esteem. Now we'll have an in-depth look at those emotions and how they are affected by the hormonal chemistry that takes place during each menstrual month.

Emotional Storms

Dramatic hormonal changes can occur during each monthly cycle, as well as throughout most of a woman's adult life. Is it any wonder that many of us experience life as sailing the ocean in a sailboat—calm and serene with gentle swells one day, then hurricane gales and tidal waves the next? Sometimes we wonder if we'll even survive.

Throughout my years as a counselor it was a well-accepted fact that certain physical changes take place within our bodies each month during our reproductive years, and even beyond. But emotional problems? Ha!

Often women would come to me with emotional problems such as extreme highs, depression, anger, and even suicidal thoughts. When I tried to relate those problems to hormonal changes, my ideas were usually shot down very quickly.

I fought for over thirty long and hard years to convince other counselors that there was indeed a link between a woman's emotional problems and her menstrual cycle and hormone imbalances. In spite of the research I'd done and the articles and books I'd collected, many of my peers refused to take my findings seriously.

Fortunately, I was not entirely alone in my thinking. In those early years of my practice, I obtained some reprints of research material from a large pharmaceutical firm, which linked emotional disturbances with hormone imbalances. That and a few additional articles from the library convinced me I was on the right track. In fairly recent years my theories have been substantiated by such specialists as Dr. Katharina Dalton, author of *Once a Month*, and Dr. Penny Wise Budoff, in her book *No More Menstrual Cramps and Other Good News*.

With these books available on the market, at last women who suffer from premenstrual tension and PMS, postpartum blues or depression, perimenopause (mid-thirties to early-forties slump), and menopause are getting help.

In the next few pages, we'll look at what our bodies do to throw our minds out of whack.

As an example, I'm going to use Jane, a 27-year-old woman. Her menstrual month is very much the same as mine used to be. Symptoms vary in every woman, but a guided tour through Jane's menstrual month will probably paint a picture familiar to most of us.

Jane and her husband, John, live with their three children in a quaint old farmhouse. They bought the farm and adjoining property with the idea of restoring it to an authentic Victorian farmhouse. Most of the time Jane is well adjusted and happy with her life. But watch as the hormone levels in Jane's body rise and fall and note how those changes affect her mood, her emotions, and even her personality. She is as predictable as the tide, yet as unpredictable as the sea.

The surging tide   When we watch the ocean's incoming tide, we see the water level rise. The sea is alive with energy and excitement as the rushing, churning waters race toward the shore.

On the first week of her menstrual cycle, just as her menses begins, estrogen advances and, like the rising tide, floods her body in preparation for ovulation. It's a passionate, energy-giving time.

Jane springs out of bed and creeps down the stairs of the old farmhouse. It's 5:30 A.M., but she feels too energetic to stay in bed. She spends a half hour in a thought-provoking Bible study and prayer and still has plenty of time to set the table with a white linen cloth and her special Blue Willow china. A bowl of blue pansies from the window box and blue mugs for milk add the finishing touches.

Jane is confident in herself and in her relationship with the Lord and all mankind. It's as though the universe is spinning to the beat of her song. "What a lovely day," she whispers. "I'm so glad I talked John into buying this place."

Jane hurries up the stairs to wake her youngsters. She pauses in the doorway to admire their angelic faces. Irritation threatens to mar her perfect day as she stoops to pick up the socks and jeans scattered about the room. But she lets the minor frustration pass; after all, it's up to her to work with them more on tidiness. *And I will*, she promises herself. She drops a light kiss on each of their foreheads as she says, "Time to wake up, darlings."

After sending hubby and the children out the door fortified with a magnificent breakfast, Jane takes a moment to make out a schedule for her day. "Let's see," she says, "I'll need to do laundry, tidy the house, bake bread. While the bread is baking, I must make those telephone calls for the women's retreat committee. Then I'll paint the cupboards, weed the garden, and find stakes to support the delphiniums. How quickly they've grown! Then I'll dash out to the farm and pick fresh strawberries."

She feels so ambitious that she ends up making out a things-to-do list for the whole month.

Jane glances at the outdated kitchen appliances, shabby brown cupboards, and dreary dining room wallpaper. The farmhouse kitchen may be run-down, but she loves the enormous size of it. Instead of its depressing her, she feels confident that within a very short time her decorating projects will be finished.

Feeling vibrant, Jane zips through everything on her list and has energy left over to calmly help the children settle their after-school squabbles. In the evening, after a luscious leg of lamb dinner served with her homemade mint sauce, Jane pops the children into bed and relaxes with her husband, who is discouraged by problems at the office. She listens and gives wise encouragement. Later she kisses hubby good night, then works late into the night, sewing curtains for the den. With all this energy pulsing through her, sleep seems a complete waste of time.

High tide The tide is in. The brimming sea pulses and moans, heady and inspiring. It is the second week of Jane's cycle, when estrogen has reached its peak and begins to level off.

Jane's driving ambition gives way to creativity. She is more likely to concentrate on a specific project. She is not the dynamo of last week, but tends to pace herself more moderately. She is still confident in herself and in her abilities and determined to reach her goals.

Jane feels especially good about her accomplishments as

Monday rolls around again. Today she will relax a little and find time to start that new herb garden near the back door. She visualizes a sundial in the center, surrounded by a bed of lavender. Fragrant thyme would make up the edging. She imagines herself gathering herbs from all over the world to fill her scented garden. Of course it will need a little white picket fence and a gate. She is euphoric as the vision becomes more and more real. Why, she could even create a business out of it.

The old place could be called "Lavender Land," and she would wear lavender smocks. Maybe she would become an expert, collect every variety of lavender known, and become the world-renowed Lavender Lady.

On Wednesday she is especially pleased with her all-day session on the women's retreat committee. It had been a big new step for her to head up the retreat, and she found she really could do it. At the large church in town, she had never dared become involved in any leadership roles. Jane feels encouraged about everything in her life.

The fertile sea   There is a time at high tide, just before the waters recede, when the sea is fertile with life, ripe for the fisherman's lure. Although the waters are never really still, there is a tense quiet as the sea prepares for its return journey.

Toward the end of the second week, ovulation occurs. Ovulation is a distinct phase in itself, as it brings on obvious changes. It is characterized by a leveling off and integrating of emotions. Jane finds herself wrapped in a sweet cocoon of peace and well-being. On the other hand, her hormones are waiting, tense and ready. Will pregnancy hold the tide on the shore? Or will the sperm fail in their task and cause the womb to discard its fetal bed?

Jane still feels good physically, although she is not quite as assertive. Relationships with hubby and children are on an even keel. This is the time of the month when most wives feel their highest peak of sexual desire—a deep, underlying urge to mate. Jane may not accomplish all the things on her list this week, but she is calm and productive and understanding of herself and those around her.

Morning finds Jane in an aura of sheer contentment. She feels calm, quiet, and serene about life and her surroundings. She stretches deep within the warm coziness of her bed and snuggles down for just a few more minutes of soothing rest. Her dreams about the house and garden are so real that the blue and cream kitchen leading into the rose colors of the dining and living room are only a wink away from reality.

Jane's heart nearly bursts with devotion, love, understanding, and acceptance toward her husband and children. She wonders how she could have ever been upset, worried, or depressed in the past. Nothing they do seems to touch her blissful state, and Jane wishes all days could be like this.

Not even the children's misbehavior can dent her serenity. And those youngsters are being particularly irritating just now. They seem to be continually fighting and are getting worse instead of better at keeping their room clean. But Jane doesn't let her concerns over the boys cloud her calm skies. She stretches and scoots herself up against the fluffy pillows. Besides, she reminds herself, boys will be boys.

She banishes any concerns for her children and smiles down at her sleeping husband. Waves of love sweep over her.

How strong and broad his shoulders are. What a dear man he is. I'm so lucky to have John's love. I wouldn't change places with anyone.

Jane lets her imagination drift back to her college days. "Please marry me," Ashley, her old college sweetheart, pleads in the soft, blurry light of her daydream.

"Oh, Ashley, how sweet of you to ask. But . . . well, I love John."

"John! Why, he doesn't even have a job. I can give you everything money can buy. I love you." Ashley drops to his knees and gives her an armful of two dozen roses.

Jane smiles and dreamily gazes at John's picture. "No, Ashley. I love John. I don't care a fig about jobs or money. My love for John is all that matters."

The daydream fades and Jane knows that her decision years ago was a wise one. John has real values. He never looks at other women, and he's kind and good-natured. He's a wonderful husband and father. He always provides for them, sometimes sacrificing his own cherished ambitions in order to have a steady income for the family. And best of all, he is a fine Christian man and an excellent role model for the boys.

Jane reluctantly sets her daydreams aside and eases herself out of bed. She doesn't particularly feel like getting up, but as always there is work to be done.

An hour later Jane kisses her family good-bye. It's a warmish day, and she feels a bit lazy. She goes to her desk and digs out her household planning book. She can't believe how much she has accomplished over the last two weeks. Today, however, she doesn't want to follow a schedule. "I am going to have a fun day off," she decides. "I'll call Polly to see if she would like to go antique hunting."

The creativity of a full and fertile sea and the integration (sensitivity and harmony) of ovulation ebb away as we move into the third menstrual week.

The ebb tide In the third week of the cycle, Jane's estrogen tide rises slightly, but not with as much force. Progesterone surges in to dominate the scene. At the end of week three, the two hormonal tides ebb and a contrary restlessness invades the fickle, retreating waters.

During the week, Jane has had several up and down days. She's disturbed because she seems to be accomplishing less and less and the dull days drag on. Occasionally she experiences a foreboding, the doldrums—like the calm before the storm.

I particularly like the word *doldrums* here because it seems to fit the scene. In tropical seas there were times when crippling storms caused havoc for the ships caught in their pathway. Just before the storm, the sailors would experience an oppressive, eerie quiet. They had a sense of foreboding and gloom. All efforts to change position were fruitless. The ship was becalmed. They could not escape the oncoming storm.

During this lull, Jane tries not to think about it, but knows what inevitably lies ahead. She is heading directly into the path of a premenstrual storm.

Not all days bring the doldrums. There are some semiproductive days, but often Jane feels self-indulgent and a bit lazy, even to the point of taking naps in the afternoon. It is almost as though she mourns with the retreating tide. The turbulent water drags her into its powerful undercurrent and swallows her spirits.

Jane's enthusiasm of the last couple of weeks seems to have vanished, and she has only enough energy to keep up with the essential daily chores without starting anything new.

The outgoing tide   During week four, we focus in on Jane a few days before menses. The progesterone and estrogen tides are receding quickly now. A tense anxiety builds as the churning sea empties into itself.

She hears John puttering around downstairs. Her nerves grate with irritation, and her head throbs in pain. "He's probably trying to make me feel guilty for sleeping in," she mutters. But getting up is the last thing she wants to do this morning. It's almost as if she's afraid of what the day might hold.

Jane finally rolls out of bed. Feeling listless and irritable, she staggers into the children's room. The little socks and jeans strewn about the room are not cute. The children awake to their mum's exclamations of, "What a mess! How many times do I have to tell you to put away your clothes? No one ever helps me around the house!"

Jane stops a moment to rub her temples in an attempt to soothe away her morning headache. She tries to hurry, but everything slows her down. Breakfast turns into another disaster as she grabs the box of fresh strawberries from the refrigerator. The box, as if it were deliberately taunting her, jumps out of her hands. She watches in tearful anger as the berries skitter across the dingy floor. Just when she needs to hurry, her hands won't cooperate with her mind.

Am I losing my mind? she wonders as she crouches to retrieve the berries. She feels as though she's disintegrating and wants to scream. *I must be going crazy*, she tells herself. *But I can't—not in front of the children.*

After what seems like an eternity, she shoves hubby and the children out the door and sits down to look at her schedule for the day. "I must have been insane to plan all this. I can't possibly get all these things done," she groans. A glance around the kitchen depresses her even more. "We'll never get this wretched place fixed up. How could I have ever let John talk me into buying it?"

She avoids her devotions, as she doesn't feel like talking to God. Guilt stalks her, but she's just not up to reading the Bible now. She remembers how Jesus calmed the sea and wishes He could calm her. But the restless sea of churning emotions inside her won't be calmed by anyone, she thinks, not even God.

"What's the use?" she moans. "I'm a failure. This morning proves it. I'm a rotten wife and mother. I don't know why I ever got married in the first place. This marriage certainly isn't working out as I had planned. Maybe I should leave—go back home. I wonder how Ashley is doing these days? What a guy. He used to bring me flowers. John never brings me flowers. With Ashley's money we'd have this house restored in no time. Maybe I should have married him, after all. No, on second thought I should have pursued my career. I'm not cut out to be a wife and mother."

It is now 11 A.M. and Jane becomes more depressed when she sees she has done nothing but bemoan her existence. Suddenly she wants something sweet. "I know what I need, a scrumptious piece of pie with cream and a cup of coffee." There is nothing left in the kitchen to meet her particular cravings, so she jumps in the car and heads for the shopping center five miles away. Here she orders apple pie with cinnamon sauce topped with real cream and a double scoop of ice cream.

The bakery smells wonderful, so Jane buys a box of assorted pastries—for John and the boys, of course. She roams around the shops, reluctant to go home. The scent of spicy Polish sausages draws her around the corner to the deli, where she samples several varieties of sausage and pickles.

On the way home she reaches into her bag and munches on an almond croissant. Once home, she is ravenously hungry again and eats another sausage and an apple strudel, washing it down with a strong English tea.

Eating has given her a spurt of energy, so she decides to tackle the much-needed repairs on the stairway, working with an almost manic fury.

As she works, Jane still harbors morbid thoughts of failure and hopelessness. Whatever made her think she wanted this stupid humdrum domestic mediocrity with a bunch of difficult kids?

Wait a minute, another voice inside seems to say. *A couple of weeks ago you were really happy, weren't you?*

Jane answers aloud, "That was a illusion, a dream. This is the real world, the way I really am. There's no use pretending anymore. I'm a failure."

By evening Jane is so exhausted that she can hardly get dinner on the table. She feels emotionally drained, shaky, unattractive, overweight, and totally lacking in self-esteem. The tide is out.

Low tide The primal waves toss their heads and thunderously explode against the ancient earth, anxious to cover the naked shore.

In low tide the waters draw back, but they are by no means still. As we focus in on Jane in the hours before her period is to start, we find her more than reluctant to get out of bed. John gathers his work clothes and plunks down on the bed to pull on his jeans. Then he reaches for his socks and jerkily pulls them on. Jane's head is pounding as a result of John's clumsy moves, and she is suddenly filled with irritation and hate for him.

"Must you bounce on the bed like that? My head is aching and . . . oh, what's the use of telling you? You couldn't care less about my feelings. You never *have* cared. No one ever, ever cares about me in this family. I hate being stuck in this country dump. This is what I get for trying to do what *you* want all the time."

"But, Jane, I always thought the farm was your dream for all of us."

"Well, I hate this mess," Jane argues. "If you really love me, you should have known I could never live like this. I wish we had never left the city."

"Jane, I wish you could have heard yourself complaining about the lack of space and the constant quarreling of our boys with the neighbor kids. You have often said our boys have changed since they got out of that neighborhood."

"You just don't understand me at all, do you?" Jane pouts.

"No. And I'm not sure I want to. Women!" John stomps out the door. "I'm sick of these stupid arguments."

"Then go find someone else," Jane yells at the empty hall.

Jane hates herself for her outburst. She hadn't really meant those things, yet in a way she had, too.

The house is quiet when she finally dresses and stumbles down the stairs. Her head aches and her hands are trembling. John had cooked bacon and eggs in the big frying pan in an annoying attempt to feed himself and the boys. Everything is slimy with grease. Dirty dishes litter the counter, and water covers the old wooden draining boards. A jug of milk has been left in the sun on the breakfast table.

Jane is so irritated she feels like biting someone. She decides to face John and the boys right now and have it out with them. Her angry, savage feelings spill over in her harsh words. "What's the idea of leaving that filthy mess for me to clean up? I'm fed up with the whole lot of you, and if anyone ever again leaves a mess like that, you'll be sorry for the rest of your lives!"

Later she hears John explain that Mum is having one of her bad days. "Let's try to be especially kind to Mum today," he says. "And for heaven's sake, stop quarreling. It might be best if we stay out of her way for a while."

It grates on her nerves to hear John say it, but maybe he's right. If she could just go off by herself for a while, she might feel better. She grabs a new antique magazine and shuts herself away in the bedroom. Jane reads only a few pages before dozing off.

Sure as the changing tide The tide wanes, then swells, throbs, and roars to flood the shore again. The incoming tide draws the waters into fullness. Just so, Jane's internal tide is drawing forth fresh hormones and changing her emotional sea.

It is 6 P.M. when Jane awakens. The headache is gone, along with the awful tension. Jane's thoughts turn to making a great supper for everyone. *Let's see—the boys adore those instant chocolate puddings, and a hot turkey casserole would be just right after all their work with their dad.*

It is then Jane discovers she's begun to menstruate. She feels a bit draggy, lethargic, and slow, with some slight cramping, but her spirits have risen and she can face the world again.

She is thrilled to see that John and the boys have finished the fencing around her new herb garben. They even made a brick path leading into the center where they'd set an adorable ancient-looking cement birdbath covered in patches of moss.

Jane is delighted. *How great to be living in this beautiful peaceful area and to have such a wonderful family,* she thinks as she hurries around her kitchen to prepare supper. *There is something very special about having a family of boys and living in the country.*

Jane's hormonal tides have risen and fallen in a cycle as old as time. Along with the rise and fall of her estrogen and progesterone, we have seen how deeply her emotional life was affected by the changing tides.

Are You Affected by Hormones?

Are you affected by the rise and fall of your hormonal tides? Not all of you will experience such obvious changes during your menstrual month. There will be women with lesser symptoms and women with worse symptoms. Nonetheless, we can see how in Jane's case the hormonal changes

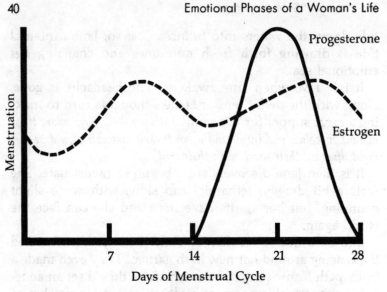

Variations in estrogen and progesterone levels
during the menstrual cycle.

that occur during the monthly cycle greatly affect her energy levels, her emotional highs and lows, and even her thoughts and family relationships.

Below is a listing showing the different phases and corresponding weeks of the menstrual cycle. With each week I've listed the possible emotional responses. Notice how closely the emotions and feelings parallel the cyclical hormonal changes shown on the diagram above. Look over the lists and circle those that most closely describe you during your menstrual month.

First Week: Rising estrogen levels
Self-directed, disciplined
Assertive: tries to motivate family and friends
Independent
Optimistic
Self-confident

Positive
Outgoing, extroverted
Has high self-expectations; maniclike busyness
Task oriented
Disciplined
Purposeful
Well focused
Very coordinated
Reasonable
Overly ambitious
Sociable
Aware of sexual feelings
(Some women carry over gloomy attitudes from fourth
    week for a short time, and then a sense of well-being
    follows quickly.)

Second Week: Estrogen levels off and declines slightly

Blue skies overhead—good, warm, summerlike feelings:
    happy, hopeful, and easygoing
Not depressed
Has a sense of well-being, inner strength
Sets more realistic goals than during first week
Less assertive—manic activities gone
Creative, with positive energy
Optimistic
Sensitive to the loveliness of the environment
Peaceful
A peacemaker
Isn't bothered by small irritations
Idealistic dreams and goals for self and family
Feels reasonable and tolerant of self and others

Ovulation: Estrogen rising again, progesterone rising

Passive, introverted
Passive receptive (submissive, patient, accepting, open-
    minded)

Sexual readiness and/or assertiveness

(Rising estrogen and progesterone mingle producing a
high level of sexual behavior. For some it is the only
time they feel sexually assertive. Others report strong
sexual urges at other times as well.)

Strong motherly feelings

Romantic and sentimental feelings toward children and
husband

Tolerant of small irritations

Accepting of self and others

Peaceful, benign

Content—satisfied and being complete—whole

Sense of being unified or integrated

Enjoying her various roles

Third Week: Rising estrogen and overriding progesterone

Subject to variable feelings: some good and some bad
days—up and down feelings

The doldrums

Moody and gloomy—a sense of feeling doomed

Apprehensive for no apparent reason

Feeling immobilized

Doubting herself

Slowing down; disliking pressure

Discouraged

Less friendly and outgoing

Losing sense of well-being

Longing for more peaceful life

Impatient with children more often

Losing interest in goals and plans, bored

Lacking coordination

Less goal oriented

Fourth Week: Premenstrual—estrogen and progesterone levels fall

Very reactive, irritable, touchy, nervous

Moody, unstable

Unable to concentrate
Sensitive to noise
Unpredictable, outbursts of emotions
Quarrelsome, impatient with husband and kids
Childlike, unreasonable
Lack of self-confidence
Loss of interest in hobbies and tasks
Not ambitious
Melancholy, withdrawn
Awkward, shaky
Food binges, craves sweets or spices especially.

(*Note:* A more complete list of premenstrual feelings is located on page 213.)

Remember, the symptoms vary from woman to woman and may even vary from month to month. Some women feel no emotional changes at all.

The above list is by no means a test, but a method of helping you become more aware of how you react to your hormonal tides. Quite a number of women, in spite of all the publicity and material available on premenstrual tension, are not aware that emotional disturbances and mood swings can be related to hormones.

Simply understanding that hormones can influence emotions has brought many of these women relief. Knowledge can alleviate the fear of the unknown and work to decrease tension. Knowledge also helps us to cope and gives us hope. But, it doesn't erase the frustration or eliminate the symptoms.

One woman came up to me after a seminar and said, "I understand that my hormones are causing a lot of my emotional problems, but I'm confused. Which week of the menstrual cycle shows the real me? I had a psychologist tell me that when I act out premenstrually, that is the way I really am. The rest of the month I'm simply more in control and covering up my true feelings. Is this true?"

This is absurd, and I told her so. Let's go back and take a look at our model, Jane. The truth is, Jane is accomplished, well adjusted, talented, goal oriented, energetic, and dearly loves her husband and children. She doesn't lose those traits during her premenstrual phase; she simply doesn't have the strength or desire to function on a high energy level all month long. When the estrogen and progesterone levels drop, so do Jane's drive, ambition, and mood.

Normally, most of us can cope with the changes in our emotions and realize "this, too, will pass." But if your emotions overrun reason and become too much for you to handle—and some women with premenstrual syndrome fall into that category—medical intervention may be necessary.

Now that we've had a look at the menses and how it affects our emotions, let's take a moment to find out why. What happens physically to account for many of those emotional storms we encounter throughout our lives?

3

The Nature
of a Woman   🦢

Carol, a woman in her mid-forties, approached me at a seminar recently. "Jean," she began, "your chart showing what happens to our bodies through the menstrual cycle really clarified things for me. I was surprised to see how closely my emotions and physical symptoms followed your example."

"Yes," I replied, "it helps to see it written out."

"I'm so glad you talked openly about it and really appreciate your taking the time to explain," she continued. "So many people just assume we know all about our bodies these days. Maybe most women do, but it's been ages since I studied sex education, and I'd forgotten some of those basic facts."

"Believe me, I know just what you mean," I said with a chuckle. "I was raised to be a proper British lady, and one absolutely did not talk about such things."

"I'm glad we're able to be more open now. Thanks again."

With sex education in schools these days, many of you are fully aware of every detail of your menstrual cycle and its biological process. Or perhaps, like Carol, it's been a long time since you had a sex education class, and you have forgotten a few of the minor details of the ebb and flow of hormones, such as where they come from and why.

Just in case you need it, I'll provide a brief review of the female reproductive cycle and how it works. You might want to take a moment to review it.

Human Endocrine Glands

Within the body are glands that produce secretions directly correlated with our sexuality. These glands are the pituitary gland, the gonads, and the adrenal glands.

The pituitary gland, weighing about 600 milligrams, is a small, bean-shaped organ located near the base of the brain. The hormones produced by the pituitary are called gonadotrophic hormones. These hormones direct changes in the production of sex hormones from the gonads. The pituitary has often been called the "master gland," as it regulates the rate of hormone production in the other endocrine glands.

Gonads are the ovaries in women and the testes in men. In men these gonads produce sperm cells. In women the ovaries produce ova, or egg cells. These gonads are responsible for producing the primary sex hormones in our bodies.

The adrenal glands, located above the kidneys, are made up of two parts, an inner section called the medulla and the outer cortex. Sex hormones are produced in the cortex only.

The word *hormone* is derived from a Greek word that means "to excite" or "to set in motion." Hormones set in motion a series of events that creates a change in the body.

Hormones are produced by these various organs and carried through the bloodstream to the appropriate organ at the appropriate time.

Few sex hormones are produced during childhood, but at the onset of puberty—around twelve for girls and fourteen for boys—the hypothalamus, a sort of control center in the brain, signals the pituitary into action. Hormones then seem to burst out all over. The pituitary hormones begin circulating through the bloodstream, causing both the gonads and the adrenals to enlarge and secrete more of their sex hormones. Women begin to develop breasts, ovulate, and menstruate. With all this hormonal activity it's easy to see why adolescence can be such an emotionally volatile time.

The Female Reproductive Organs

The female reproductive organs include the ovaries and the uterus. They are located in the lower abdomen. The uterus is a fist-size organ that opens into the vagina through the cervix. At the top end of the uterus are two extensions called fallopian tubes, which open to the ovaries.

The ovaries are filled with 100,000 to 400,000 immature egg cells. Each of those cells is enclosed in a group of cells called a follicle. The ovaries take turns in producing an egg cell ripe for fertilization each month.

After puberty the pituitary gland releases a follicle-stimulating hormone (FSH) that causes one of the immature eggs to ripen. Thus the menstrual cycle begins.

As the egg ripens, the follicle grows larger. The growing follicle produces estrogen. This estrogen causes the mucous lining of the uterus (called the endometrium) to become thick and engorged with blood. If the egg is fertilized, it nestles into and attaches itself to this soft enriched lining and finds nourishment from the blood. When the egg is not fertilized, part of the endometrium sloughs off, along with some blood, at the beginning of the cycle.

The Monthly Cycle

The cycle begins with the flow of blood as the endometrium sloughs off. The menstrual flow signals the beginning of a new rise in FSH to ripen a new egg cell.

As the cell develops, the follicle grows and produces rising levels of estrogen, as indicated in week one on the chart. About two weeks after menstruation, the high levels of estrogen trigger a release of luteinizing hormone (LH). This hormone causes the egg follicle to burst and release the mature egg cell, which travels into the fallopian tube. The LH works on the fallopian tubes to draw the egg cell into the uterus.

Once ovulation has occurred, body levels of estrogen and LH drop sharply. Meanwhile, the burst follicle becomes a yellow substance known as corpus luteum. The corpus luteum secretes another hormone called progesterone. Progesterone helps to maintain the lining of the uterus.

Intercourse during the ovulation phase may result in pregnancy, as sperm will travel from the vagina, through the uterus, and into the fallopian tubes. Only one of the thousands of sperm is needed to fertilize the egg.

Should fertilization occur, the egg adheres to the uterine lining, where it is nourished until the placenta is formed. Progesterone continues to be produced by the corpus luteum, maintaining pregnancy and suppressing the secretion of FSH. (As you recall, FSH gets another egg ready.)

If the egg is not fertilized, it won't attach itself to the uterine wall. Consequently the uterus no longer has to be prepared for pregnancy and the corpus luteum stops making progesterone. When the progesterone level falls, the uterine lining breaks down.

At this point another substance enters the scene—prostaglandin. When the progesterone stops and the endometrium begins to break down, prostaglandins (which are produced in the uterus) arrive on the scene to help expel the uterine contents. Prostaglandins do this by causing the uterus to contract. During the contraction there is a lack of circulation in the uterus, which may cause cramping.[1]

As the uterus contracts, it rejects the lining and the unfertilized egg, causing the menstrual flow. The average length of flow from the uterus is about five to seven days. Day one of the cycle begins with the beginning of blood flow. The length of the cycle varies in individuals and may even differ monthly for each woman, but a typical cycle will run in twenty-eight-day to one-month intervals.

The reproductive phase of a woman's life from puberty to menopause usually lasts some forty years. At around fifty years of age, the thousands of eggs are gone. Only about one percent of all those eggs mature and make their way to the uterus. The others are lost through a degenerative process called atresia. After this gradual loss of the eggs is completed, the woman enters a phase in her life called menopause.

This simply means she stops menstruating. At this time, the body undergoes some significant changes. Estrogen is no longer produced by the follicles, and the corpus luteum stops providing progesterone. The changes women undergo at this time can be very dramatic, possibly even more so than those occurring at puberty.

With all this chemistry going on, is it any wonder our bodies behave strangely at times? It's easy to see how the tiniest upset in the ebb and flow of hormones could cause even the healthiest of us to capsize occasionally.

4

Sometimes
It Hurts ... _____ ᕀ

There are times when being a woman just plain hurts. At any age from puberty to menopause, menses can be the source of extreme discomfort.

Discomfort is a little too mild a word to describe one woman's feelings about her menstrual periods. In a recent phone call, Helen said this:

> My symptoms start about a day before my period and get worse the first day or two that I flow. It starts with severe muscle pain in my back, especially my shoulders and neck and sometimes in my upper arms, chest, and breasts. I get a dull pelvic pain, reminiscent of labor pains (I have six children). I often have nausea, diarrhea, bloating (I feel like I've gained ten pounds). In general, I feel like I've been run over by a truck!
>
> The thing usually runs its course in about four days. My patience grows short, I'm irritable, but usually not hateful. Emotionally, I'm coping, although at times I'm under a lot of stress.

My son, Dr. David Lush, a noted family practitioner, tells me that Helen, along with millions of other women, is suffering from a condition called *dysmenorrhea* (painful menses).

"It's Not in My Mind"

Most doctors today readily recognize and are willing to treat the physical discomforts that occur with menstruation.

According to a pharmaceutical publication titled "Painful Periods," dysmenorrhea is the most common cause of lost work or school hours among women in the United States. It is estimated that 42 million women in this country suffer from painful menstrual symptoms. Of these, about 3.5 million have symptoms so severe that they are unable to function for one to two days each month.

Some very real changes are taking place in the body, and they can be quite uncomfortable. Most painful periods are a result of normal body functions and are not generally harmful. Occasionally, however, there may be complications.

For example, there is a condition called *secondary dysmenorrhea*. Here the cramping is a result of an abnormal physical problem or disease. A cervix that is too small can act as a dam and block the menstrual blood. Or the problem may be a disease in the uterus such as endometriosis, where deposits of endometrium grow in the wrong place. Usually these conditions can be easily diagnosed and corrected by surgery or medication. Secondary dysmenorrhea requires a doctor's care.

Most painful menses (where there is no abnormality or disease) are called *primary spasmodic dysmenorrhea*. This discomfort is part of the normal menstrual cycle. Symptoms can include spasms or laborlike pain in the lower abdomen and back during menstruation. There may be pain and pulling on the inner thigh. Women will occasionally complain of nausea, vomiting, diarrhea, dizziness, fainting, and headaches. A woman may experience one or more of these symptoms for between six hours and three days of her menses. Why? Prostaglandins released into the bloodstream at or toward the end of the luteal phase just prior to menstruation are responsible for menstrual cramping. The higher the levels of prostaglandins, the more severe the pain.

Another example of menstrual misery is called *primary congestive dysmenorrhea*, which is generally diagnosed when a woman complains of abdominal discomfort before menstruation. This usually goes along with bloating, breast tenderness, and premenstrual tension. These symptoms will begin anywhere from two to fourteen days before menses and disappear when the flow begins or shortly after.

Both of these problems are called primary dysmenorrhea because they appear as a result of normal body function. They are not considered harmful and can usually be treated.[1]

As you can see by reviewing the reproductive system, most women—simply because they are women—experience some discomfort with their changing hormones.

5

The Good News Is ... ———— ॐ

With menses, some discomfort and emotional ups and downs are normal. That's the bad news. The good news is, you can get help.

In chapter one I talked about the importance of maintaining a healthy amount of self-esteem as we make our journey through womanhood. Another suggestion that may help reduce the severity of symptoms, especially the emotional ones, is to stop feeling guilty over the way you may have acted or spoken during your premenstrual time.

Overcoming Guilt

Women will often feel they have let themselves, their families, and even God down. They beat themselves with invisible switches because they are not being spiritual enough, or busy enough, or sweet enough.

Positive and negative emotions are a part of our being. God created emotions in us—all emotions. Unfortunately, sometimes we act out those emotions in a hurtful way.

Beverly, who is 42, has a wonderful way of dealing with the negative feelings she experiences prior to her period.

When I go through those irritating days—miserable days—I withdraw from people as much as possible. When I blow it by getting angry or unreasonable, I'll ask forgiveness as soon as I can think straight again and feel confident it's over and I can go on. I also make sure my family knows that there may be times of the month when I blow things out of proportion. I ask them to help me by staying out of my way and by trying to understand what I'm going through.

I work hard to remember I'm forgiven. The other thing I do is to pamper myself.

Pamper Yourself

Beverly continues:

Those days before my period, I take special care of myself. I don't push myself to accomplish much. So what if the house goes without being vacuumed or dusted? It will keep. I conserve my energy for the important things, like trying not to let my feelings overcome my good sense.

I also take that time to do quiet, relaxing things. If I have cramps or a headache or just don't feel good, I'll take aspirin and rest. I take frequent luxury baths, read, and go off by myself whenever I can.

I usually release built-up tension by writing out my feelings in a diary or journal. Sometimes I'll spend the day at the library, write letters, or go to a movie or symphony. Other times I'll treat myself to dinner out or go on a two- or three-day trip (that doesn't happen often, but it's nice). I try not to schedule anything demanding during that time.

I guess it's kind of like listening to my body and working with it, instead of against it.

Beverly isn't the only woman who finds help in working *with* her body. Stress can be greatly reduced when we stop fighting our bodies and let go. Some women I've interviewed say that when they pamper themselves and take special care of themselves during their premenstrual time, the dark days when the tide is out seem shorter and less severe.

One woman said:

> For years I couldn't understand why I felt so energetic and capable one week and totally inept the next. I tried so hard to keep up the energy level, but I failed miserably. Then one day I said to myself, "What the heck?" I took the day off and did nothing. I decided not to feel guilty, and didn't. I let myself be me. What a difference. I'm a changed woman. I discovered a sensitive, deeper person in those quiet times. I write poetry and read the Psalms and always find something encouraging.

Whether you suffer only mild premenstrual tension or severe PMS, or fit somewhere in between, I encourage you to try both these suggestions: maintain freedom from guilt, and pamper yourself.

Painless Periods

Dysmenorrhea can be treated in several ways.

Many doctors suggest that we continue our normal activities as much as possible. Staying in shape and maintaining our health is always good advice. Exercise has been found to relieve cramping for some women.

When prostaglandins are the cause of menstrual pain, relief has been found by using prostaglandin inhibitors. Although this may sound rather technical, these drugs are ones you've all heard of. Aspirin, Motrin, and Nuprin, to name a few, have all been used successfully to reduce the discomfort of menstrual pain.

Recently my son and I were discussing PMS, painful cramping, and the appropriate medication.

I said to him, "Looking back on my own experience with PMS, I suffered with violent headaches. Other times I'd be doubled over with cramps. I remember one day those terrible cramps hit me during a field experiment. I was working with a number of brilliant scientists and wanted very much to hide, but had nowhere to go. We were involved in a controlled experiment and were assigned to plant wheat.

"There I was on my haunches, in extreme pain, wishing I could lie down or even just hold my stomach. But I had to plant this wheat within the allotted time. I couldn't tell anyone—especially those men—about my problem. In those days you just didn't talk about it. So I had to suffer in silence and keep up with all the other researchers."

"Actually, Mom," he responded, "if you had known it, two or three aspirin would have probably cut that discomfort by two-thirds."

"Yes, but we didn't know that."

"A lot of people found out accidentally that aspirin helps cramps. It works better than codeine or Demerol."

"So you recommend aspirin for premenstrual and menstrual pain?" I asked.

"Sure," he concluded, "as long as my patient can tolerate it."

We are indeed fortunate to have medications at our disposal in these modern times. But before you take any antiprostaglandins, even aspirin, check with your doctor.

In addition to the antiprostaglandin therapy, Dr. Joe McIlhaney suggests using heating pads and warm baths to increase the blood flow through the abdomen and relieve cramping.[1]

Occasionally, birth-control pills are used to control painful menses. According to Dr. McIlhaney, dysmenorrhea, in the absence of PMS, can and often has been relieved by using birth-control pills.[2] With the pills, the uterine lining is thinner and less prostaglandin is manufactured. Consequently the uterus contracts less and there is less cramping.

As you can see, there are various helps for those who suffer from painful periods. I would suggest, however, that instead of treating yourself, you work with your doctor to decide which method of treatment is best for you.

Part II

The Romantic Phase — 🦢

The second emotional phase of a woman's life is what I like to call the romantic phase. It includes women from about twenty-five to thirty-five years of age. This phase is not romantic in the sense that all is right with the world, but women in this age group often hold on to romantic, idealistic dreams.

It is a time in our lives when we find ourselves adapting to our chosen roles. It is a time for beginning careers, falling in love, getting married, and having babies.

Some of us are married and into the task of rearing children, others have chosen the single life with a career, and still others are awaiting their Prince Charming. In the following chapter, we'll be exploring the delights of motherhood, the flaws in fairy-tale thinking, high ideals, and great expectations.

There is nothing romantic about some of the hormonal imbalances and emotional upheavals that can creep up on unsuspecting women in this phase. In chapters seven and eight, we'll drop from the castle tower into the moat as we explore some problems that often befall women in their early childbearing years: postpartum blues, postpartum depression, PMS, tubal ligations, and hysterectomies.

Chapter nine offers current information and suggestions to help you even up the odds in your battle against hormonal distress.

6

Great Expectations — ໖

Phase two of our lives is quite often greeted with pleasant anticipation. We want the best out of life and plan to get it. A woman in her twenties and thirties will often have irresistible enthusiasm for her new role. She tends to find fulfillment by striving for perfection.

In this and the following chapter we will be concentrating on married women with children and their particular problems.

To illustrate, come with me into the delightful world of Gwen, mother of three-month-old Elizabeth and two-year-old Lance, Jr.

Fairy-Tale Beginnings

This phase of life is a time of fairy-tale beginnings. Prince Charming is probably still a prince, though his armor may be a bit rusty. And dear, unsuspecting Gwen ponders the Utopian dream of carrying out her role of being the greatest wife and mother in the world.

Gwen is sure she'll make that goal. It is almost as if she

has a built-in recording that says, "If I do well in these roles, life will be good. I will live happily ever after. My dreams will be fulfilled in my husband and children as I make them happy."

As Gwen cares for her home, husband, and children, her expectations and idealism run high. She is trusting and hopeful, often too busy and too involved with her goals to see danger signals in the lives of her children, husband, and herself. She often ignores or rationalizes away difficulties in her marriage and family and follows an idealistic theory that says all will be well as long as she plays her part. Rather than deal with a problem, she will more likely excuse it or cover it up. Even escorting young and strong-willed Lance through his two's may not change Gwen's castle-tower view of life.

Gwen's reluctance to see the real picture is understandable. After all, admitting to problems in her home might indicate that she wasn't doing a good job. And that would never do for a princess.

Fulfilling Expectations

Along with Gwen's own ideas of being the greatest wife and mother in the world come the expectations of society. Culturally, the wife and mother is the giver in the family, as well as in the community. She must give up many of her own needs and desires in order to meet the needs of those she loves. There are expectations placed on her by her husband, her demanding young children, her parents, her church, and community.

In addition, many young women are expected to work at full-time or part-time jobs to keep the family finances from going under.

So our young mother generally ends up running in high gear, constantly chauffeuring, grocery shopping, cleaning, cooking, playing the role of a happy, loving wife and mother, and perhaps working as a business executive.

Gwen, like many other women in the romantic phase, has a storehouse of energy and can easily become entangled in the web of busyness. She's doing double duty, and eventually it will catch up with her. If a woman is prone to being a supermom, this is usually the time she succumbs.

This is of concern because high-stress situations and overloaded working schedules can have a tremendous bearing on our fluctuating hormones. It is well documented that stress worsens the symptoms of premenstrual tension, premenstrual syndrome, and postpartum depression, the primary causes of emotional and hormonal problems in this age group.

Oddly enough, it is often the change in hormones that initiates some of the supermom mentality. Remember our model Jane, and her emotional high the first week of her menses? She really believed she could do anything—and for the moment, it was true. But remember, too, what happened to her great expectations a couple of weeks later. Just as Jane's hormones brought her up, she also experienced a hormonal change that resulted in the great fall out of Utopia.

I wouldn't ask you to give up goals and dreams; on the contrary, some dreaming is necessary to survival. Optimism and a self-sacrificing attitude certainly have their places throughout our lives. But idealism and extremely stressful situations can cause some serious problems later on.

While we continue to cushion ourselves against too many hard realities with our romantic view of life, we must retain a glimmer of realism as we approach each phase of our lives. That touch of reality can do wonders to help us grope through the dark nights and stormy days of postpartum blues or premenstrual tension. Knowledge of these possible problems can prevent us from ending up in the castle dungeon wondering why our rose-colored world suddenly went dark.

As we journey through the emotional phases of life, we will do well to remember that there are no perfect people or places, not even in romantic fairy tales. There are always black knights, dragons, witches, towers, moats, dungeons, damsels in distress, and princes who turn into toads.

7

Distressing News: Postpartum Blues 🐦

Shelly held six-pound Joshua in her arms a few hours after birth.

"He has your dimples," Shelly said as she smiled lovingly at her husband, Tom.

"Yeah, and he has Uncle Joe's hair."

"Tom," Shelly gently stroked the fine strands of hair on her baby's head, "Uncle Joe doesn't have any hair."

"Right," Tom grinned. "But I guess I shouldn't tease the little guy. I'm sure his hair will grow in—won't it?" He watched in admiration as his son's tiny hand closed around his finger.

"Of course. Just give him a little time."

"Time!" Tom jumped to his feet. "That reminds me, I've got to pick up Mother at the airport. I'd better get going."

"I'm so glad she could come and help. But would you straighten up the house a little before she comes? I'm afraid we left things a mess."

"Relax, honey. Mother and I will have everything all

ready for you and the baby. You'll have complete maid service."

For the next two weeks Shelly delighted in the dozens of
oohs and aahs over her new baby. Presents and cards
poured in, and the world was painted a rosy glow. Tom's
mother handled all the meals and laundry, giving Shelly
plenty of time to rest and get acquainted with little Josh.

Finally, Tom's mother boarded the plane, the visitors and
presents stopped arriving, and Shelly looked forward to
settling down with her sweet family. Then it happened.

She'd felt the tension building inside her for a few days,
but dismissed it. Now the tensions and stress poured down
on her like bricks from a demolished building. She dialed
her friend Debbie's number. As soon as Debbie answered,
Shelly's tears came.

"Shelly, what's wrong?"

"I don't know. I feel so awful. I don't understand it. I've
got a new baby, and he's so good, but I'm terribly depressed. What's wrong with me?"

"Oh, Shelly," Debbie's comforting voice reached through
the wires. "I'm sure it's nothing to worry about. You've
probably just got a case of postpartum blues."

Shelly sniffed. "I do?"

"Sure. I remember going through it with two of my kids.
It only lasted about a week with the first, then I didn't have
it at all with the next two. With Andy, my fourth, I was depressed for three months. Don't worry; it will eventually go
away. At least mine did."

Debbie was right; Shelly's symptoms disappeared after a
few days. But what caused her depression?

Pregnancy, Hormones, and the New Mom

The fertilization of an egg brings about an obvious shift
in hormones. Levels of progesterone remain high through-

out pregnancy, giving Mom a comfortable feeling of well-being. The body is preparing for the birth of the baby. In this stage a woman feels natural nesting instincts. Concern for the baby and its welfare are uppermost on a mother-to-be's priority list. She works throughout the pregnancy to make certain the baby will have a safe, secure place to live, investing much of her time and talent in preparing for motherhood.

Once the baby is born, the mother's body goes through another drastic change. Another hormone, prolactin, which is responsible for milk production, comes on the scene. As prolactin levels increase, progesterone levels drop. Under normal circumstances, this hormonal shift after pregnancy shouldn't last for more than a few weeks.

How does the shift in hormones affect Mom's emotional level? Many new mothers will go through a phase called postpartum blues, which is quite normal. As in Shelly's case, it is brought on by the normal shift in hormones following birth and also by the stresses of adjusting to the new baby.

One would think that having a new baby would be the most exciting time of life. After the baby is born, there is a romantic, euphoric feeling. Then, before long, Mom typically ends up in a fit of crying spells. She's suffering from postpartum blues and finds it extremely hard to cope. The darling baby wets, messes, and spits up all over the place. Her stitches hurt, her breasts are painful and engorged. Hubby still expects meals on the table, and baby may even develop a case of colic.

Mom is up half the night meeting the demands of this anything-but-peaceful doll. The natural letdown of expectations, along with the change in hormones, leads to postpartum blues. To add insult to injury, all too often the new mom will end up feeling guilty.

Most of the time, postpartum blues give way to a happy, well-adjusted life with a normal monthly menstrual cycle.

Postpartum Depression

There are a few women, however, who develop more severe and prolonged symptoms of depression following the baby's birth. This longer, more serious problem is known as postpartum depression (PPD).

Postpartum depression and premenstrual syndrome have been found to be very much the same problem. The difference is that PMS is cyclical, occurring before each period. PPD is continuous, not changing with menses. PPD is often more difficult to diagnose than PMS because of the lack of cyclical changes or symptoms.

Often the young mother with PPD will not be diagnosed until her menses begins and the symptoms evolve into a monthly pattern, which may not happen for six or seven months.

I mentioned earlier that when the baby is born prolactin levels increase and progesterone drops. If prolactin levels are extremely high, one might see PPD symptoms. It is not the high prolactin, however, that causes PPD, but the low progesterone.

According to Dr. David Lush, "It's not been my experience that breast-feeding moms have terrible postpartum depression, and I would never suggest drying up a mother who wants to nurse. Consequently, I would rather use progesterone suppositories—which would rarely be necessary, and only if her prolactin levels were unusually high—than stop a mother's milk supply."

Symptoms of PPD include tired, tearful feelings with low self-esteem and the inability to cope or keep up with other people's demands. A woman with PPD might withdraw into herself with the baby, neglecting everyone else (including hubby). Or she might do just the opposite and love her husband so much the baby is neglected.

One of the symptoms most helpful in diagnosing PPD is atypical depression: The mother wants to sleep all the time. She feels totally exhausted and can literally sleep around the clock. (With new moms this is impossible, as most of us know.) With normal depression, a person can't sleep, even when genuinely tired. Mothers with postpartum depression don't necessarily need the sleep; they *want* it.

Symptoms may begin at birth or a few days after, as a continuation of normal postpartum blues. The symptoms may also begin with a return to birth-control pills, because the progestin in the pills will aggravate any depressed feelings.

Women who have experienced PMS prior to pregnancy are more likely to suffer from PPD than those who haven't.

Note: PPD is not to be confused with the postpartum blues that many new mothers get when their progesterone level drops. PPD is only diagnosed if it's continuous, abnormal, and long lasting.

In treating severe PPD, some doctors will use natural progesterone suppositories, yet many doctors believe there is no scientific evidence to validate this treatment. It is better to work with your doctor in trying dietary changes such as reducing intake of caffeine and sugar and increasing intake of vitamin B_6, vitamin C, calcium, and magnesium in appropriate doses. True PPD is treated in much the same way as PMS, once it has been diagnosed.

I'd like to give you an example of a young woman who suffered from PPD and didn't realize it until she was finally diagnosed as having PMS.

Adele says:

I began having children when I was seventeen, and by the time I had my third child at twenty, I hit a postpartum depression that didn't lift for—I don't know—I call it my black years. I probably had two and one-half years of feeling so heavy I couldn't lift my head off the table.

I wanted to sleep all the time. I was really fretful. I was actually frightened of going to the store. My husband would come home and I'd cry, "Please go! I can't. I just can't!" I was literally housebound. I had three babies and was nursing two of them.

I remember sometimes waking up in the middle of the night and grabbing my husband and saying, "You've got to take me to the hospital." He would pray with me and we'd go back to sleep and I'd make it through another night.

After my fourth baby was born, I finally began having periods again. After about six weeks, I noticed my symptoms occurred just before my period. The depression, wanting to kill myself, getting angry and hateful of life—I was absolutely freaking out. Once I started flowing, I was all right. So I said, "Hmmm. There must be a connection here."

After doing some reading and keeping a monthly chart, I was eventually diagnosed as having PMS and realized that what I had had all that time was postpartum depression.

When I went to see my doctor with my charts and everything, he suggested I try a vitamin B_6 shot first, along with the recommended dietary changes for treating PMS. I didn't really want the shot—it hurts. I had a hot pack on it all day and cried like a baby, but it helped. Since then I've been trying to get enough B_6 in my food. I also stay away from caffeine and try to stay on a hypoglycemic diet.

I still have some symptoms, but no suicidal thoughts, and I don't really freak out anymore. I can handle it.

If you think you may be suffering from postpartum depression you'll want to talk with your doctor and become informed about the symptoms and treatment for PPD and PMS.

Premenstrual Syndrome and You — ಕ

"My baby was almost three before I quit nursing," Mary, a 40-year-old mother of four, confided to me. "I wanted to give it up sooner, but I just couldn't face going back to my monthly cycle. It was awful—like walking into a nightmare, only worse. PMS isn't a nightmare you can wake up from. It's real."

What would make a woman so fearful? Before you dismiss her as paranoid, perhaps you'd better hear her story:

My awareness of PMS became very profound in my mid-thirties. Prior to that I had PMS but didn't even know it.

I generally had a few bad days every month, but assumed this was because of personal problems. When I became aware of this condition, I realized that those times when I became extremely angry and waged war with my husband were usually before my periods.

In my mid-thirties I became very angry at my husband one evening. Outraged, I sprayed him in the face with an aerosol can, which, unknown to me at the time, contained a lye product that temporarily blinded him. Then I went outside and damaged his "hobby" truck and drove the family car over a bank.

After I calmed down, I realized something very serious was happening to me. After much prayer and thinking, I came to the realization I had PMS. I'd known about PMS, but for some reason until that day, I hadn't connected it with what I was experiencing.

Just knowing why I feel like I do at the time prior to my periods has helped me keep on top of my feelings and avoid serious outbursts like the one I mentioned.

The onset of PMS is very profound and sudden for me, occurring about ten days before my period. I generally start with an increased sense of anxiety. After a day or so, this anxiety turns to a feeling of urgency and then to extreme restlessness.

Then after several days I become very angry. This anger is usually directed toward my husband or close family members. Along with the anger comes frustration and discontentment, then mood swings and depression.

These PMS days are a particularly trying time in our marriage because this is generally when I find myself dipping into a pool of past wrongs. I bring up a lot of unsettled issues and arguments and wave them at my husband like red flags. The results are always negative and destructive.

I often find myself either experiencing insomnia or else sleeping too much.

The onset of a period brings a slow but steady feeling of relief. Within about twenty-four hours after my period begins, I become aware that I feel normal again.

My family could set their calendars according to my cycle. It isn't easy for any of us to deal with, even though they realize what I'm going through. I find we can all get caught up in the problems that are created during this time.

It is especially hard for my husband—even though he is aware of why I act the way I do.

Fortunately, Mary's condition is improving. Let's take a closer look at PMS. Is it fiction or fact? What is PMS? What causes it? And who has it?

Is PMS for Real?

For Mary and a few million other women, PMS is certainly real. It is probably the most talked about, most advertised female problem ever. But we've only just begun hearing about it in the last few years.

You may be wondering why we are just learning about it now. Is PMS a symptom of our times?

Hardly. Over 2,000 years ago a Greek poet wrote this *Essay On Women:*

> She has two different sorts of mood.
> One day she is all smiles and
>   happiness . . .
> "There is no better wife . . . nor
>   prettier."
> Then, another day, there'll be no
>   living with her.
> You can't get within sight, or
>   come near her
> Or she flies into a rage and holds
>   you at a distance
> Like a bitch with pups,
>   cantankerous and cross with all
>   the world . . .
> The sea is like that also.
> Often it lies calm and innocent
>   and still . . .
> Then it will go wild and
>   turbulent . . .

> This woman's disposition is just
>   like the sea's
> Since the sea's temper also
>   changes all the time.

>   Simonides

Women apparently suffered premenstrually then, and they unfortunately still do. Up until recently, premenstrual syndrome remained untreated and generally unrecognized. Even today there are extreme differences of opinion. Because of conflicting studies and a lack of enough scientific evidence, doctors remain hesitant to deal with women who come to them with symptoms of PMS.

Doctors began talking about PMS as a medical issue around 1914. Since then only a handful of doctors have considered it worth studying and trying to come up with methods to treat distraught women all over the world.

Some doctors still resort to calling PMS a psychosocial phenomenon that has simply been sensationalized through media coverage. More and more doctors have accepted PMS as a real medical problem, but not all of them will treat it or even know how to treat it.

According to Dr. David Lush, "Doctors don't like to base their treatments on what appears to be the case. They want hard, fast scientific proof—and treatment of PMS by medical intervention has not been proven. That will probably take another fifty years."

Consequently some doctors refuse to treat PMS because they fear malpractice suits. Others continue to pacify distraught women with antidepressants or tranquilizers, or send them off to the mental ward of a local hospital for a "rest."

Not only do some doctors refuse to treat PMS, but there are a few physicians and psychologists who won't even recognize PMS as a bona fide medical or psychological problem. To do so, they claim, would result in giving chauvinistic men a tool to use against women, claiming them to be incapable of making decisions or holding leadership positions because of their monthly "crazies."

For example, Patricia Shriner Ingles, a psychologist in human sexuality who was participating in a major research project at Mt. Sinai Medical Center in New York, said in a recent interview, "Studies using the most up-to-date methods show that hormones have such a small effect on our emotions, behavior, and intellectual capabilities that it's not really significant."

She went on to say, "If hormones affect women's moods, we should be able to see that easily. Women with high levels of estrogen should behave differently than women with low levels of estrogen. That didn't turn out to be the case."

Dr. Ingles found that women's beliefs and expectations were much more important than their hormone levels. The research led her to believe that premenstrual complaints were largely a conditioned response. After all, their studies showed that both men and women experience highs and lows that fluctuated with mood changes.

She concludes that "if a mother hands her daughter a feminine product with one hand and a pain reliever with the other, the mother can establish a self-fulfilling false prophecy that menstruation is an illness."[1]

Dr. Shriner Ingles does have a couple of valid points. It's true that many women can and do react in conditioned responses; they will often respond to the menstrual cycle in much the same way their mothers did. In addition, men very commonly have mood swings, but that hardly disproves the reality of PMS.

It seems a bit ridiculous, doesn't it? How can people,

especially doctors, disclaim a condition that is so evident in the lives of millions of women?

Aside from the so-called liberated women who claim that acknowledging PMS would cause even more discrimination for women, we have other doubters in the ranks. Many women who have never experienced PMS tend to discount it and are unsympathetic to those who do. Often women who have PMS deny it, thinking a good wife and mother, a real Christian, would never act or think like a PMS woman. With that kind of thinking, is it any wonder the gray cloud of confusion never seems to lift?

This confusion leaves many doctors wondering, "Is PMS simply a problem of our day, brought to mind by the media and a few drug companies that want to sell another product?" Today we have a multivitamin just for PMS sufferers that costs about $21 per 100. We also have various pain relievers especially formulated for women who suffer from PMS. Are these drug companies playing on the weakness of a few million hypochondriacs?

Premenstrual syndrome is real enough to warrant several national support groups for PMS sufferers. One such group is called PMS Access (P.O. Box 9326, Madison, WI 53715). According to PMS Access literature, there are at least two million women in America today who, largely because they themselves are victims, believe in PMS.

PMS Is . . .

Premenstrual syndrome has had many names. Some have called it a psychosomatic illness, others suggest it may be a "fad diagnosis," while others say it is a hormonal imbalance.

I've seen a lot of definitions of PMS, but I think perhaps the best is one I adapted from a pamphlet called "Premenstrual Syndrome Relief," by Gillian Ford, a PMS counselor:

Premenstrual syndrome is a hormonal deficiency disease that is characterized by a clustering of symptoms in the premenstrual phase and an absence of symptoms in the postmenstrual phase.[2] Some women only have symptoms a few days before their periods. Others may complain that they have only one good week a month, which generally corresponds with the week between the end of the menstrual period and ovulation.

In PMS, the *timing* of the symptoms is much more important in the diagnosis than the *type* of symptoms.

A Look at the Symptoms

An estimated 150 symptoms have been associated with PMS. While I won't list them all here, I can give you a rundown on the most common. See the *Appendix* for a complete list. To clarify the symptoms, I've broken them down into two categories, physical and emotional:

Physical	**Emotional**
Migraines	Irritability ⎱ almost
Nausea	Lethargy ⎰ always
Dizziness	Depression ⎱ present
Eye problems: conjunctivitis, sties, and visual disturbances	Feeling out of control
	Uncontrollable rage
Skin problems: acne, boils, hives, oral and genital herpes	Paranoia
	Suicidal impulses
	Violent outbursts
Respiratory problems, including: asthma, allergies, recurrent flulike symptoms, hoarseness, tonsillitis	Desire to flee
	Feeling of being a split personality
	Anxiety attacks
Repeated bladder or yeast infections	Phobic symptoms: fear of crowds
	Crying jags

Physical	**Emotional**
Hemorrhoid or varicose vein flare-ups	Occasional mental problems Feeling worthless Feeling guilty[3]

Just looking at this list can help you understand the complex nature of PMS. Amazing, isn't it, that even such things as hemorrhoids and asthma can be linked to PMS?

"I have a hard time buying this," one woman commented as she examined the list. "Why do men and children have these symptoms?" She's right. Anyone—man, woman, or child—can experience most of the conditions on this list. But as I said earlier, it isn't the symptoms but the *timing* of the symptoms that counts in PMS.

For instance, Elaine, a PMS sufferer, called me shortly after I had an interview on Dr. Dobson's show, "Focus on the Family."

"I have suspected for years that a fluctuating estrogen level was the culprit that brought on my allergy reactions," Elaine said. "It happens about every fourteen days, but do you think I could get a doctor to listen? My current doctor is sympathetic, but I need more than that. At least he didn't prescribe Valium for my 'female nerves,' like others have done in the past."

"Yes," I answered, "I'm certainly glad of that."

"I'm also afflicted with severe headaches," she went on to tell me, "swollen sinuses, and pain in my facial bones—my nose gets ice-cold. I have difficulty sleeping, aching eyes, blemished skin, and a lack of coordination, making it difficult to sew or write.

"Your interview with Dr. Dobson gave me new hope that maybe I can finally get some help. Could these symptoms I'm having every month possibly be PMS?"

"It could," I said. "I'm not a doctor, so I can't make a diagnosis, but it certainly sounds suspicious to me."

I went on to give Elaine the name of a doctor in our area who worked with PMS patients and put her in touch with a PMS support group.

The allergic reaction and other symptoms Elaine described could be a physical manifestation brought on by a hormonal change during her menstrual cycle.

"In 1948," Katharina Dalton says in her book, *Once a Month*, "I came across my first case of premenstrual asthma, which responded successfully to treatment with progesterone. Before a month had passed a further case of asthma, two of epilepsy and one migraine had been found, all related to menstruation."[4]

I'm not saying, of course, that all illnesses are somehow related to hormones, but many are.

No one suffers from all of these symptoms, and every woman will have a different pattern of symptoms. Some women have very few physical symptoms, while others have a great many. Doctors who work with PMS patients say the key they use in making their diagnosis is that these symptoms are *cyclical*.

PMS: The Cause

Now let's have a quick look at what causes a normal, loving, intelligent, caring woman to turn from a sweet Ms. Jekyll to a monstrous Ms. Hyde just prior to her period.

According to a May 15, 1985, *Postgraduate Medicine* article, the cause of PMS is still unknown.[5]

However, there are a few theories, which include:
- Psychosomatic causes—psychological in origin
- Fluid retention—increased sodium level may contribute to weight gain, bloating, headaches
- Low blood sugar—hypoglycemia
- Excess prolactin—a hormone excreted by the pituitary gland

- Stress
- Vitamin deficiency
- Progesterone deficiency

None of the above theories by itself accounts for the many and varied symptoms of PMS. They all seem to be pieces of a puzzle with some parts still missing.

The one thing we do know for certain is that PMS can strike anyone with a menstrual cycle.

Even a Queen Can Get PMS

PMS is no respecter of persons. As I mentioned before, it has been noted in Katharina Dalton's book that Queen Victoria of England suffered from severe bouts of PMS.[6] Mary, whose story we just read, has a degree in sociology and is a doctor's wife. PMS knows no racial or geographical barriers; it affects women all over the world in every culture and economic atmosphere.

I hesitate to use percentages here because they vary so greatly, depending on who's doing the studies and what their criteria are, but I did find some that I felt were fairly accurate. According to the PMS experts who wrote *PMS and You*, approximately 40 percent of all women between the ages of 14 and 50 experience PMS. Of those 40 percent, about 10 to 12 percent have symptoms so severe they cannot continue normal daily living.

In an article in *Patient Care*, a journal for primary-care physicians, a study showed that "the incidence of premenstrual tension syndrome varied according to age: In the early teens about 15 percent of women have some degree of PMS, and its incidence progresses to a peak of 60 percent in women age 30–40. Although the overall incidence is roughly 50 percent, only about 5 percent–10 percent of those affected have a severe, incapacitating form of the disorder.[7]

There is some evidence to show that certain conditions or experiences make some women more prone than others to PMS.

• Pregnancy complications such as miscarriage, toxemia, and postpartum depression are often followed by PMS symptoms.

• PMS symptoms tend to worsen as a woman grows older.

• It appears that married women generally suffer more with PMS than single women, and women often see their symptoms worsen after the birth of each child.

I'm quite interested in this third observation. Isn't it just possible that single women, even though they have stresses from their jobs, tend to have fewer PMS symptoms because they have fewer relationships to contend with?

Think about the wife with small children. She has multiple relationships to consider and must experience a good deal of stress in simply trying not to act out during her premenstrual time. She has no quiet apartment to go home to and must be around her family day and night, unless she locks herself in the bathroom or exiles hubby to the couch.

I remember one of my mother's friends sometimes going to bed for four days when she "came on unwell." Today's mothers seldom have that luxury. The burden of extra relationships may have a very definite effect on the severity of PMS symptoms.

• Finally, PMS symptoms seem to appear or worsen after a tubal ligation or hysterectomy.

Tubal Ligations: Are They Safe?

Tubal ligation is a means of sterilization. There are several methods used, but the end result is the same: The fallopian tubes are cut and tied, or sealed by cauterization, bands, or clips.

Tubal ligation is usually an effective, and with a laparoscopy (sometimes called Band-Aid surgery), a fast and easy method of birth control. Many women think it's the wisest decision they've ever made and have experienced no complications whatever.

However, there are some things the doctor may not tell you. The surgical procedure may have a direct effect on the blood supply to the ovaries, decreasing the hormone supply. This may be the reason for so many complaints following a tubal. While tubals are an excellent means of birth control, there are some things you should know before having one.

• PMS symptoms may increase.
• Depression may occur and last several months. For lack of a better answer, women are often told, "Your depression is because you're mourning the loss of the babies you'll never have." Most women I've talked to say that just isn't so.
• It may be responsible for irregular ovulation or uterine bleeding.
• There is danger of infection.
• There is a 1 to 3 percent failure rate in preventing pregnancy. That's not bad, but a tubal, like anything else, isn't foolproof.

Hysterectomies: an Easy Way Out?

About a year ago a colleague of mine suffered a bout of heavy uterine bleeding between periods. Her doctor flippantly said, "Well, if this keeps up, we'll have to take the old uterus out." My friend was appalled that he'd even suggest it. She'd had one previous incident of severe bleeding several years before that had been easily controlled by a couple of weeks on a mild birth-control pill. As it turned out, the same medication stopped the problem again, and she hasn't had a midcycle bleed since. She's hesitant, however, to return to a doctor who seemed a little too eager to sterilize her.

Some women are given a rosy picture of hysterectomies "taking care of things"—no more worries, no more cares. That's simply not true. Women who have had hysterectomies, even though their ovaries may be intact, complain of an increase of hormone-related symptoms. While there will be no more babies and no more bleeding, there will be hormone fluctuations and changes when the ovaries are left intact.

At one point in my practice I realized that a majority of my female clients coming in for marriage counseling had been married for around twenty years. A large majority of these women reported having had hysterectomies about two years before. In many cases, their marriages began deteriorating after their surgeries.

In addition, I've had frequent calls from women who suffer severe depression, hot flashes, no desire for sex, along with a myriad of other symptoms after having hysterectomies. One woman who phoned the other day said, "I knew I wouldn't be having any more periods and was thankful for that, but I didn't know I'd be having all this trouble."

I felt these posthysterectomy problems were occurring much too often to be a coincidence and decided to check it out. My medical resources turned up some very interesting observations.

"Depression is a common aftermath" of a hysterectomy, claims Dr. Penny Wise Budoff in her book, *No More Menstrual Cramps and Other Good News*. "It usually occurs within three to six months after surgery and can be severe enough to require institutionalization."[8]

Dr. Katharina Dalton of England also recognizes the incidence of depression in posthysterectomy patients. In a paper on "The Aftermath of Hysterectomies," she states that "44 percent of women had either been divorced, separated or had sought the assistance of a marriage counselor since the operation."

She reported the incidence of two types of depression, *cyclical depression* (which would correspond to PMS-type symptoms), and *continual depression*. In addition, Dr. Dalton cites two studies reporting a high incidence of delayed depression, happening two to three years after surgery. Whether or not the ovaries were removed had no effect.[9]

The following are some of the possible complications of hysterectomies and or oophorectomies (removal of ovaries).

• Surgical removal of any part of the reproductive system causes an irreparable break in hormonal pathways. For example, just because the ovaries are left intact doesn't mean there won't be an estrogen deficiency. Most of the blood supply for the ovaries is supplied by the uterus. When the uterus is removed, the blood supply drops and the ovaries can't function properly. They may go into shock for a time until other sources of blood increase to compensate. They may continue to supply estrogen, but their finely tuned system now has a major flaw. The hormones may be released erratically, causing depression, mood swings, and any number of other hormone-related symptoms.

• The woman's menstrual clock receives a shock.

• Changes are sudden. If ovaries are removed as well, the body goes into immediate menopause.

• Some previous PMS sufferers will go six to twelve months symptom-free, then cyclical PMS symptoms may return and be worse than before. Unfortunately, a woman who's had a hysterectomy often gets little or no sympathy. Since she no longer menstruates and still has her ovaries, she, her doctor, her family, and friends may mistakenly believe her symptoms are psychological.

• Depression is greatest if the woman is under forty years of age.

• Narrowing of the arteries and coronary vessels can increase fourfold. The presence of estrogen in the blood is extremely important in preventing this.

• Women experiencing a surgical menopause may have hot flashes, backaches, and depression. As if that weren't enough, these symptoms are often accompanied by weight gain, fatigue, and loss of energy.

With these complications arising out of hysterectomies, it isn't difficult to see why marriages break up and women feel their world is falling apart. Depression creates a terrible strain on both the husband and wife. If you are a posthysterectomy casualty, take heart. These troubles will pass in time. In the meantime, explore every possible avenue open to you, including medical intervention.

And to those women who have not had a hysterectomy, Dr. Penny Wise Budoff says, ". . . it's time women know they can choose to keep their bodies intact. Many uterine conditions," she adds, "that supposedly 'call for' hysterectomy can be treated with medication or lesser procedures."

Dr. Budoff cautions us not to be mislead when a doctor talks about a precancerous condition. A precancerous condition does "not necessarily lead to cancer at all. At the very least," she warns, "women need a specific diagnosis and a second opinion before considering a hysterectomy."[10]

When hysterectomies are necessary—and many are a lifesaving measure—consideration should be given to hormone replacement. Naturally, the woman having both a hysterectomy and an oophorectomy (sometimes called a complete hysterectomy, where both the uterus and ovaries are removed) will go into immediate menopause.

Unfortunately, it may be difficult for a woman having a complete hysterectomy to get the hormone replacement she needs, because generally the ovaries are not removed unless a life-threatening condition such as cancer is found. If hormone therapy is restricted, she may need to explore other methods of treatment with her physician.

You might wonder, with all these complications, why any woman would choose to have a hysterectomy "just in case" or because the doctor thinks it "might be a good idea." The truth is, women aren't told about the aftermath of hysterectomies. If they were, perhaps we'd have fewer healthy uteri removed and far less emotional turmoil in women's lives.

I do wish doctors would take more care in explaining the possible emotional aftermath to their patients. Of course experiences are varied, and there are a lot of women who, after having a hysterectomy, claim they never felt better.

9

PMS: Making it Better   ॐ

The romantic phase of our lives can be a delightful experience. It can be like basking in the gentle warmth of the sun and watching strawberries plump into juicy, sweet fruit. But all too often our hormones act up and make us feel as if all our fruit has rotted. The twenties and thirties can be the most exciting and the most frustrating years of our lives.

But *Emotional Phases of a Woman's Life* was written not only to inform you of possible hormone imbalances and corresponding emotional turmoil, but to offer help.

Coping With PMS

Remember Mary from the last chapter? Below is a list of the coping mechanisms she uses in dealing with PMS.

I'm always aware of where I am in my monthly cycle. I try not to be hit with the onset of PMS unexpectedly. By being aware, I can warn my family when my moods take a swing for the worse.

I try to reduce stress as much as possible. This is hard to pull off with four children and a husband who works day and night. I also try to limit my own expectations of what I should accomplish during this time.

More recently, I've tried to change my eating patterns. I reduce my coffee and chocolate intake and increase my protein intake. I also eat smaller portions at more frequent intervals.

For the past six months, my husband, who's a doctor, has administered a shot of 100 mg. pyridoxine (vitamin B_6) about two weeks before my period.

For the past couple of months I've also been using progesterone suppositories, and I feel better. But I found that it delays the onset of my period.

"None of these things totally cures the problem," Mary admits. "But they certainly do help reduce the intensity of my symptoms and allow me to feel in control again."

Let's take a closer look at Mary's list of treatments and changes, plus others that women have found helpful in controlling PMS. My son, Dr. David Lush, and I have put together a step-by-step list of suggestions that may give you the answers you're looking for.

Be Willing to Change

Effectively dealing with PMS may require months of dedication to record keeping in order to validate the problem and pinpoint specific symptoms. It requires an honest look at yourself, your life-style, your medical and psychiatric background, and your personality.

Finding the right treatment or series of treatments can be a trial and error type of program requiring much effort and time. Successful therapy may even require that you be willing to change your habits and life-style.

PMS patients often have a high failure rate, simply because they lack the willingness or willpower to change. Believe me, I understand that; discipline and willpower are not easy to come by. Yet if it would help reduce the severity of PMS symptoms, maybe even stop those crazy, out-of-control days, wouldn't it be worth a try?

One of the first steps on our list is to see a doctor.

See Your Doctor

If you are now suffering from what you think might be premenstrual syndrome or postpartum depression or another form of hormonal imbalance, I'd suggest you visit your gynecologist. This is especially true if you are having heavy bleeding, pain, erratic periods, or other symptoms that might indicate a serious medical problem.

Maybe you don't have a doctor, or perhaps you have one who doesn't seem interested in working with you on your PMS problem.

Before you write your doctor off as uncaring, go a step further. Ask how he or she feels about treating PMS. Many physicians are reluctant to treat PMS because they are trying to provide a balance in the care they give their patients. In one medical journal, doctors are advised to "keep abreast of current developments and rational treatment—while serving as a buffer against medical fadism."[1]

Their fears are not invalid. The press coverage PMS has had, as well as public opinion, can cause women to jump to conclusions about the medical care they think they should have.

There are many doctors who, because PMS is such a clouded issue, prefer not to deal with the myriad of symptoms it presents, and that's okay—sad, but okay. You won't want to go to a doctor who isn't well-read on the issue, anyway. We have a lot of specialists these days, and you'll simply have to search for a doctor who will work with you.

Maybe you've tried and simply can't find the right doctor for you. In that case, you can get a list of doctors knowledgeable in treating PMS and other hormonal disorders through a PMS support group, PMS Access, P.O. Box 9326, Madison, WI 53715.

Maybe you have a doctor who cares, but you are frustrated because he or she doesn't seem to be working fast enough or isn't giving you what you think you need. In that case, I'd suggest you be patient and follow the steps outlined below. For further help, PMS Access has a kit they sell to their subscribers, titled, "How to Approach Your Doctor."

Gain an Understanding

The next step is for you to gain an understanding of the problem and the available medical treatment. We've discussed some of the factors surrounding PMS: its definition and some possible causes. I have only been able to give you a brief review of the subject. If you believe you are a PMS sufferer, you will want to write to one of the PMS support groups and start gathering more information.

We also saw that PMS is not an easy illness to treat because of the complexity of symptoms. So, with Dr. Lush's help, let's look at some methods of treatment and potential problems from the medical standpoint.

Dr. Lush says, "Basically, hormone imbalance in PMS is going to result in hypoglycemia, fluid retention, depression, and low self-esteem. You need to look at all the symptoms and try to correct them."

One of his patients, a 32-year-old woman who suffered from severe postpartum depression and PMS, said, "Everything in the body seems to go haywire, and you just have to see where the most sensitive areas are and where to hit on it."

Dr. Lush continues:

You've got to understand the trouble with medicine. I can sit in my office and show a woman a graph of her monthly cycle. I can show her pictures of red and blue eggs popping out of follicles and show her lines to indicate the levels of estrogen and progesterone. Then she can tell me how she feels. I can compare her symptoms with my experience with other female patients.

But I'm not going to be able to order a test that will tell me the levels of anything. I'm not going to be able to measure her prostaglandin, estrogen, or progesterone levels at that moment in time and be able to make a diagnosis based on those levels.

So, what I have to do is look at the big picture. I know that her entire body is affected, because the hypothalamus governs all kinds of systems in the body. She can tell me she is bloating and gaining two or three pounds of body fluid. She can tell me she has a headache or that she is suicidal and go through a complete list of other symptoms.

The whole business makes PMS a complicated medical problem. It isn't surprising that a lot of doctors don't want to deal with PMS patients.

It would be very nice if we had one medication that would correct all these things, but we don't. We're talking about a total body system being affected, and we have to approach it with a variety of plans and treatments.

We know there are no miracle cures, no one plan for alleviating the symptoms of PMS. So where do we start? How do we reduce the complexity of PMS down to terms we can deal with?

Keep a Diary

Dr. Lush advises, "Before a woman even attempts to seek her doctor's advice on reducing the symptoms of PMS or

PPD, she should keep a diary." And he adds, "If a woman comes to me complaining of symptoms, I'll do a preliminary examination to make sure nothing else is wrong. I wouldn't want to miss a diagnosis of a tumor, endometriosis, infection, or the like. If everything checks out, I'd probably send her home to keep track of her symptoms for about three to six months."

But, you may be asking, wouldn't some doctors be offended if a woman came in with a chart and had already diagnosed herself as having PMS?

"I wouldn't." Dr. Lush says, "I really appreciate it when a woman has taken the time to become informed and has already done her homework. The diary helps me find the problems more readily. We can see the pattern and know better what we're dealing with. I can get to the methods of treatment faster."

A chart and diary can help put you in closer touch with your body. With them, you can more accurately measure what your symptoms are and determine whether or not those symptoms are cyclical.

Below is a chart that can help you measure your monthly symptoms.

Date	Jan	Feb	Mar	Apr	May	Jun	Jul	Aug	Sep	Oct	Nov	Dec
1												
2												
3												
4												
5												
6												
7												
8												

Date	Jan	Feb	Mar	Apr	May	Jun	Jul	Aug	Sep	Oct	Nov	Dec
9												
10												
11												
12												
13												
14												
15												
16												
17												
18												
19												
20												
21												
22												
23												
24												
25												
26												
27												
28												
29												
30												
31												

M = Menstruation	Ba = Backaches
H = Headaches	Bl = Bloating
D = Depression	I = Irritability

In each square, mark any symptoms you may have. Obviously you can't write them all in such a small area, so you'll want to create your own code. To do this, first make a list of your worst symptoms.

For example, say you have headaches, bloating, irritability, backaches, and depression. Simply assign each symptom a letter and code it at the bottom of your chart, as shown on the sample.

Follow the days of your cycle closely. At the end of each day, chart any symptoms you experienced. In addition, make a note in a diary of how you felt that day. Be sure to indicate your good moods, your achievements, and positive feelings, as well as recording those bad days when everything seems to go wrong.

Some of the materials I've read advise women to keep a record of their "bad days," or "attacks." I'd like to see women note the positive days, as well. Too much emphasis on negative feelings can lead to more depression. I think it's important, especially on your horrid days, to be able to turn back the pages in your diary and say, "Look at all I accomplished a few days ago," or, "I really had a good time with the kids last week." These positive days can help you cope better with the rough times ahead and make them less devastating.

Your daily diary page may look something like the one on page 95.

Naturally you won't fill out every line every day, but journalizing like this can help you get a handle on your feelings and even help alleviate some of your stresses.

Reduce Stress

It takes a tremendous amount of energy to maintain a home and raise a family. Add to that the stresses of an outside job plus symptoms of PMS, and you have the elements

Date:_____   Day of cycle_____

Feelings and day's events:_____
_____
_____
_____
_____
_____
_____
_____

Dietary information (What you ate, how often. List cravings. Did you stick to your diet? Did you blow it?):_____
_____
_____
_____
_____
_____
_____

Problems or stresses and how you handled them:_____
_____
_____
_____
_____
_____
_____

of a time bomb. Many women today are in high-stress jobs, and their home usually isn't any less stressful.

Since stress can have a detrimental effect on both hormone balance and emotions, it seems only logical that in reducing stress on our bodies, minds, and emotions, we can perhaps lessen PMS symptoms.

With all we modern women have to do, how can we reduce stress? Working women can hardly call the boss and say, "I'm taking a few days off to relax." Or could they?

Personally, I think we all could use a monthly day off. Some offices actually have "mental health days." In addition to one sick day a month, the employees get another day off, a mental health day.

So often we are encouraged to save or accumulate our sick time or days off. Maybe we should treat those days like gifts and feel free to take them when we need to lessen the more severe PMS symptoms.

Here are a few more suggestions:

Meditate   Meditation isn't just for gurus and cults. It is a very acceptable and quite Christian thing to do. Have you ever gone off by yourself for a few hours and spent time alone with God? Try it. Perhaps you'd want to spend some time reading the Bible. Maybe you'd like to pray. Or maybe you could do nothing.

I have a friend, Lois, who finds tremendous relief in meditation. "Sometimes I walk to the park or find a quiet place where I can watch the trees, flowers, and birds. Sometimes I talk to God, and sometimes I just sit still and listen. After awhile I can feel the tension slip away."

Take bubble baths   The bathroom is a great little hideaway. One mother of eight says she'd never have survived without one. "I always did my reading there," she admitted.

"There'd be days when I knew if I heard *Mom* one more time, I'd shove my fist through the wall. That's when I'd tell the kids they were on their own and head for my private domain. I'd take a long, hot bubble bath and before long I could uncurl my fists."

Get a baby-sitter One of the chief complaints among mothers of small children is that they can never get away. Hire a sitter on those days when you need to be alone. If money is a problem, make a deal with another mother or ask the children's grandparents to watch them while you rest.

Nancy, a young mother of three, told me about her feelings of frustration. "I get so angry with the children sometimes, it scares me. The other day Andy, my four-year-old, dropped a glass in the sink and I went into a rage. I shook him and sent him to his room. It really scares me when I get like that. I'm afraid I'll lose control and hurt the kids."

"Why don't you get a sitter and spend a day shopping or doing what you like?"

"What?" She gasped. "Hire a baby-sitter for that?"

"Why not?" I asked.

"Well, because. I'd be too embarrassed to ask someone to take care of the kids just because I'm . . . what would I tell them? 'Could you watch my kids while I try to cope with the crazies?' Besides, I can manage, and hiring a sitter would be a selfish use of money."

"Nonsense!" I countered. "What if you were suffering from a serious illness? Let's say you've had a heart attack. The doctor says you mustn't exert yourself. Would you ask for help? Would you hire a sitter occasionally to give your heart a rest?"

"Well, of course, but . . ."

"PMS is a potentially serious condition affecting both

your mental and physical well-being. Women have been denying it for years, but it still exists. Taking a break to keep from screaming at your kids is as essential to your health as resting after a heart attack."

Most of us, like Nancy, spend much of our lives nurturing others, but rarely do we take the time to nurture ourselves. I've talked with a lot of women who feel they are not entitled. I find this especially true of busy mothers. Too many women have confused loving and caring for themselves with selfishness. We need to learn how to consciously give ourselves permission to take care of ourselves.

Relax with your favorite music Music has been known to "soothe the savage breast." Set aside the guilt you feel because you could be doing something constructive, put your feet up, close your eyes, and listen.

Write I mentioned before how journalizing can help to clarify thoughts and put life into perspective.

Read This is a good time to give yourself permission to read that book you've been wanting to get into for ages, but never had the time to read.

Exercise Find a form of exercise you can live with. Walk, do aerobics, swim, bike, run—the list goes on and on. But whatever form of exercise you choose, spend at least thirty minutes a day doing it, preferably at the same time each day. Working out relieves tension, improves blood circulation, and generally makes you feel better.

Sometimes bloating, cramping, depression, and fatigue can curb your exercise regimen. Sometimes you will need to slow down, but generally you'll want to maintain your exercise program to the degree possible, even when you don't feel like it.

Keep your schedule loose Before you make appointments and decide to take on a major project, consult your menstrual calendar. Try to schedule the heavy, demanding jobs during your first and second weeks. Taper off as you slide into the third and fourth weeks. Learn to listen to your body. After all, would you deliberately throw a party on the night before an important test? Of course not. Likewise, it doesn't make much sense to subject yourself to a high-stress situation when you know you are heading into PMS.

Dietary Changes

This has got to be one of the hardest treatments to carry out, yet it is the most obvious place to begin and has often been found extremely effective.

Hypoglycemia (low blood sugar) and fluid retention are frequently found as part of PMS. Both these situations can be at least partially treated by dietary changes, so let's have a look at what those changes in diet involve.

Hypoglycemia occurs in many women premenstrually. This is a situation where blood sugar falls quickly or is at a low level. It is interesting to note that the symptoms for hypoglycemia often coincide with PMS symptoms. They include: depression, fatigue, insomnia, anxiety, headaches, irritability, and dizziness.

Oddly enough, the hypoglycemic diet has also proven helpful to women with PMS whose laboratory tests didn't indicate a low blood-sugar level. It is also important to note that even though the symptoms only occur premenstrually, the diet should be maintained throughout the entire cycle.

Dr. Michelle Harrison's book, *Self-Help for Premenstrual Syndrome*, contains the basic principles of a diet for PMS victims. They are as follows:

• Eat whole grains, nuts, and seeds, instead of refined sugars and flours.

• Drink no caffeinated beverages (coffee, tea, colas). Drink plenty of water, but no decaffeinated tea or coffee.

• Instead of three large meals a day, eat small amounts frequently. Every two to three hours, have a snack or small meal.[2]

Below I've listed the basic foods that should be eaten and those to avoid.

Foods to Eat
Whole grains
   Unsweetened granola
   Rye
   Wheat
   Bulgur
Fruits (high fiber/low sugar)
   Apples
   Berries
   Pears
Legumes
   Garbanzos
   Lentils
   Kidney beans
   Green peas
Seeds and nuts
Green leafy vegetables
Root vegetables
   Carrots

Turnips
Rutabagas
Oils
   Corn and safflower
   Olive
   Sesame
Foods to avoid
Caffeinated beverages
Dairy products
Chocolate
Sugar
Alcohol
Beef, pork, and lamb
Salt and high-sodium foods
Fruits (high in simple sugars)
   Oranges
   Grapefruits
   Papayas
   Pineapples

I can't go into complete dietary plans here, but I can direct you to several sources of more detailed information:

   Self-Help for Premenstrual Syndrome, by Michelle Harrison, M.D. (Matrix Press, P.O. Box 740, Cambridge, MA 02238).

   Premenstrual Syndrome Self-Help Book, by Susan Lark, M.D. (published by the PMS Self-Help Center).

Some of the problems associated with hormonal imbalances may be caused by the poor eating habits many women fall into. Many women are in a constant state of dieting to lose or control weight. Diets, especially fad diets, can cheat the body out of the vitamins and minerals needed for good health.

Vitamin B_6 Therapy

"One vitamin B_6 shot was all it took and I was back to normal." Debbie, a 32-year-old woman with four children, had been suffering severe symptoms of depression premenstrually. "It was like a miracle. I've never had to have another one. But I thank God for that, because that shot hurt *so* bad."

"Is that all you did?" I asked her.

"Oh, no. I think my body was really low on it. In fact, I wondered at the time if I really had PMS. Maybe the lack of vitamin B in my system just made my symptoms worse. Anyway, since then I've been really careful about my diet."

"Are you symptom-free now?"

"No, I still have some premenstrual tension, but I can handle it."

Cases like Debbie's, where one treatment had such a profound effect, are rare. But vitamin B_6 (200–800 mg./day)[3] along with other B-complex vitamins, has been helpful in relieving symptoms of depression and bloating for some women. However, I must caution you here. Vitamin therapy is not to be taken lightly. As with any medication, there is a danger of overdose.

An overdose of vitamin B can lead to serious and severe side effects, which can include nausea, headache, dizziness, restless sleep, and nightmares. Vitamin B_6 should be balanced by using other B-complex vitamins.[4]

Before you place yourself on a vitamin and mineral regimen, study the different vitamin and mineral groups. Learn what levels are safe for you. And, of course, consult your doctor.

Minerals Your Body Needs

Calcium and magnesium have been shown to relieve premenstrual cramping in some instances. According to my sources, the mineral supplement is taken premenstrually in doses of 250 mg. of calcium and 250 mg. of magnesium daily.[5] Again, it would be wise to contact your doctor before beginning your own therapy.

Vitamins and minerals are necessary to the body, whether or not you have PMS or other hormonal problems. Potassium is also essential to our bodily function.

One of the symptoms of low potassium can be fatigue. Your best source of potassium is in foods such as nuts, grains, fresh vegetables, and fruits. More specifically, potassium is found in bananas, dates, lemons, artichokes, avocados, Brussels sprouts, parsley, spinach, beans, parsnips, potatoes, rice, wheat, almonds, dried coconut, peanuts, sesame seeds, and sunflower seeds.

Oil of Evening Primrose

Romantic sounding, isn't it? Oil of evening primrose contains an essential fatty acid called gamma-linolenic acid, which is found in human milk and the seed oil of evening primrose. It has been found to relieve several PMS symptoms, particularly breast tenderness and swelling.

Michelle Harrison, M.D., the author of *Self-Help for Premenstrual Syndrome*, recommends a dosage of .5 gram twice a day, increasing slowly to 2 grams twice daily if needed. It does cause gastric irritation, so it should be taken with food.[6]

This nonprescription substance is available in most pharmacies and health-food stores. But I would caution you: Allergic reactions may occur, and it has been known to cause migraine headaches in women who are prone to alcohol-induced migraines.

Antiprostaglandins

I mentioned the use of antiprostaglandins in connection with painful periods. These drugs include aspirin, Motrin, Ponstel, Naprosyn, and others. None of these has actually been approved for the treatment of PMS, yet many doctors have used them with success in treating the physical symptoms of breast pain, bloating, premenstrual pain, and joint pain. They apparently have little or no effect on emotional symptoms.

Tranquilizers and Mood Elevators

As I talk with women about PMS and the treatment recommended by their doctors, the question of tranquilizers and antidepressants often arises. I have spoken to many women whose doctors have prescribed mood elevators and tranquilizers. Fortunately, overuse and abuse of tranquilizers such as Valium have received much publicity of late, and doctors are being more careful about using such addictive drugs. But many are still relying on antidepressants to treat depression in PMS patients.

Actually, this type of therapy has not been very effective and can even be detrimental. One expert source says, "psychoactive drugs should not be used in PMS treatment unless an underlying psychopathology [a mental problem] is present."[7]

Diuretics: Do They Really Work?

Diuretics, better known to most of us as water pills, have been widely prescribed in PMS treatment. They remove fluid from the body and reduce bloating. Although there are no conclusive studies to prove diuretics work, many women who have been given diuretics showed significant improvement in mood and weight reduction.

Diuretics must be prescribed by a doctor and used with caution. While diuretics may help, they also may produce side effects such as lethargy and a general malaise (not feeling well).

There is a natural diuretic that can be used without much worry—water. Drink lots of it. Water can actually reduce bloating by stimulating your kidneys to eliminate excess water and salt. Other natural diuretics include raspberry leaf tea, chamomile tea, cucumbers, and watermelon.

Progesterone Therapy

While many PMS experts agree that progesterone therapy is the key to relieving PMS in some women, there is still a lot of controversy and misunderstanding over the drug.

Even doctors who often use progesterone in the treatment of PMS are careful not to prescribe the drug too freely and will often try other methods first. Why? Because it is a drug and because its side effects have not been proven. There is much confusion over the safety of progesterone. Some animal studies indicate progesterone increases the risk of cancer and breast tumors, yet some progestational agents have been used to treat cancer.

To be on the safe side, physicians generally use progesterone as a last resort, when the PMS symptoms are severe enough to be life-threatening or interfere with a normal life-style.

Dr. Katharina Dalton, a British gynecologist, has been treating PMS since 1948 and can probably be considered a leading authority in the use of progesterone. She has prescribed progesterone to thousands of Englishwomen and has gotten what she calls excellent results.

In the United States, the Food and Drug Administration refuses to approve progesterone as therapy for PMS. But then, according to my research, they haven't approved *any* drugs for the treatment of PMS.

There are other valid concerns over progesterone use. Progesterone breaks down rapidly and can't be taken orally. It must be administered via painful injections or through rectal suppositories. The suppositories can be inconvenient and cause irritation to the surrounding tissue. Some women develop a tolerance to the drug and need increasingly larger doses.

In addition, progesterone is expensive, costing anywhere from one to five dollars per suppository or injection.

Other side effects may include: a longer or shorter menstrual cycle; spotting premenstrually or at mid-cycle; erratic cycles; increased menstrual cramps; heavier or lighter bleeding; a change in sex drive; euphoria, faintness, headaches; addiction.

One of the more serious problems arising from progesterone therapy has been that many well-meaning doctors have inadvertently prescribed a synthetic progesterone rather than the natural one.

One woman, Theresa, 36, suffered from severe PMS symptoms. Two weeks before her menses she would become hateful toward her husband. She complained of being tired all the time and wanting to stay in bed. She also talked of having out-of-body experiences.

"I can't even have normal conversations with people. My sister and I aren't speaking. We had a blow up over—I can't even remember what it was. She has PMS, too. Anyway, I can't control my screaming. My husband tells me to settle down, but I can't. I feel really bad because I lose control. Then I hate the world and think everyone is against me and I'd be better off dead. It's a terrible feeling.

"Sometimes people would come to see me and I'd hide in the closet because I didn't want to have to deal with the problem. I wanted to be left alone."

"Did you have any physical symptoms?" I asked.

"Yes. I don't think I went one time without headaches. I also had some mild cramps and breast soreness."

"And your symptoms were cyclical?"

"For the most part," she replied. "I knew they were some-how connected to my period, but when I'd ask my doctor, he'd shake his head and say, 'No way.' "

"How did you finally get help?"

"Actually, my mom had seen or read something about PMS and called me. She said, 'This sounds just like you.' Then I started looking into it and did a chart. I took it to my gynecologist and pleaded with him to give me progesterone. He said he knew I had PMS but was reluctant to treat me. He finally gave in and handed me a prescription.

"I took the pills he prescribed and got worse. I couldn't understand what was going on. I was so sure progesterone would help me. Then I went to another doctor and found out I'd been given the wrong stuff—a synthetic form of the drug."

"What approach did this new doctor take?"

"Well, I told him what I'd been through, and he told me I should never have been given the synthetic progesterone. Then he examined me and went over my chart and agreed that I should try the progesterone suppositories. I was on them for four months, and it helped tremendously. I'm not crazy anymore."

Unfortunately, doctors will sometimes prescribe birth control pills for PMS sufferers. These contain progestogens (or progestins), which in some cases may be the worst treatment for a woman with PMS symptoms.

Natural progesterone is manufactured in human bodies and can also be found in soybeans and yams. It is generally prescribed in doses ranging from 200 mg. to 400 mg. daily.

Progesterone has helped some women. Even so, it is not the miracle drug of the century. Some women find it doesn't work at all for them, while others obtain more relief from dietary changes, stress reduction, or vitamin B_6 therapy. The point is, everyone is different, and what works for some won't necessarily work for others.

PMS sufferers are finding help, even if they have to wander through this maze of treatments to do so. As I said earlier, finding the treatment right for you, your body, and your particular symptoms may take months.

Join a Support Group

Support groups for PMS sufferers are springing up all over the country. If you aren't aware of one in your own community, you might want to start one.

One woman from a small town put an ad in the local paper and started a group with ten women.

Within a group of peers, women can share feelings, be open and honest about their episodes of anger and depression, and discuss how they feel about their husbands and children. The participants can feed one another suggestions for coping, as well as gather up-to-date information on PMS. These groups have proven to be a rich resource for the community as a whole in understanding PMS and its far-reaching effects.

Part III

Mid-Life Malaise ___ ஜௌ

In the middle phase of our lives, from about ages thirty-five to forty-five, our marriages and careers have generally settled into a routine. This is a time when many women question their life choices and ask, "Is that all there is?"

In chapter ten we'll talk about some of the emotional turmoil that accompanies mid-life, the symptoms of the late thirties to early forties slump, the need for self-fulfillment and romance, the emptying nest, restlessness, and fall-apart marriages.

Then in chapter eleven we'll cover the premenopause phase and discover some hormonal fluctuations that just might be behind some of problems we women experience in mid-life.

Chapter twelve will offer suggestions to help you survive the various emotional and physical symptoms of the mid-life phase.

Chapter thirteen will be devoted to regaining your mystique in order to build self-esteem, put romance and excitement back in your life, and become the kind of woman your man can't resist.

10

Is That All There Is? _____ ૭∾

In the last section, I warned young women in the romantic phase of life about the dangers of too much fairy-tale thinking and high expectations. Too much romanticizing and idealism can lead to great disappointment when you reach your middle years.

All of us come into mid-life with different backgrounds and ideals, so our approaches to growing older will vary. I'd like us to take a look at one woman's life: Ruth, who is now 38 years old. For the last sixteen years Ruth has been operating in high gear, working part-time as a waitress, caring for three children and a husband, cooking, cleaning, chauffeuring, and so on. Since her marriage to Joe, she's hardly had a minute to call her own. Ruth has been busy playing the virtuous role of Happy Homemaker, better known in recent years as Supermom.

I've chosen Ruth because her romantic phase reflects that of many women who have come to me for counseling over the years and have attended the various women's seminars where I speak.

Ruth was raised in a Christian home. She was trained to believe that wives have certain roles and are to act a certain way. She is a wonderful mother and wife, a pillar in the home and community.

Let's take a moment to review a brief outline of the expectations Ruth tried to meet.

Ruth was trained to be a giver. Her output role (what she does for others) heavily outweighs her input role (what she does for herself).

She faces high expectations from:

• Herself, causing her to develop a supermom mentality.

• Her peers, with whom she feels she must compete.

• Her husband, who not only expects his lovely Ruth to be a submissive little homemaker, but also to contribute to the financial well-being of the home by working as a waitress.

• The church and society, whose high ideals for a wife and mother are written clearly in the faces of everyone she meets.

Ruth believes that her years of sacrificial support will eventually bring her a "happy ever after" life—someday—if she tries hard enough.

High expectations and pressure to be eternally self-sacrificing pushed Ruth into high gear and extreme busyness throughout her romantic phase. Let's pop in on Ruth and see how she is doing as she emerges from romance into mid-life.

Ruth's twenties were full of dreams and disappointments. The energy level so prominent then is now waning. Ruth's children are becoming increasingly independent. Days that used to be filled with caring for them seem empty and long. Now she has more time to think, to reevaluate and consider how far she has come and what life is all about. Ruth, now approaching forty, doesn't necessarily like what she sees.

Through the Looking Glass Darkly

These days, I'm almost afraid to look in the mirror. The woman looking back at me is a complete stranger. She has wrinkles and a few gray hairs. She looks drab and tired much of the time. I feel as if my image is mocking me, saying, "Look at yourself. You've put in thirty-eight years, and where has it gotten you? You gave up an exciting career with the airlines to marry Joe and raise a family. At first it seemed like a good idea, but not anymore. There must be more to life than this. Let's get out of here." My image compels me, "Leave this ungrateful family of yours and go have a good time while you still can."

At first I didn't take those thoughts seriously, but—and this is the frightening part—my reflection is beginning to make sense. More and more, I long to escape. I know it's selfish, but I want to go somewhere where I'll be appreciated, do something for me, and maybe find someone who can really meet my needs.

I'm not sure what my needs are. I just feel empty . . . hungry for something. I want to be taken seriously. I want love. Is it wrong to expect a little romance in life? I want to be happy again and full of energy. These days it's all I can do to haul my carcass out of bed. I keep thinking if I get away, I'll somehow find what I'm looking for.

"I used to feel that way many times in my early forties," I told her. "There were times I desperately wanted to run away to Australia. I'd fantasize about becoming a recluse and letting others care for me. I didn't do it, of course. When it came down to the packing, I knew I couldn't possibly leave my family."

"Oh, I couldn't leave mine, either," said Ruth. "I feel guilty just thinking about it. I love my husband and children, but . . . well, sometimes I feel like I've been drained of every ounce of love, strength, and caring I had in me. I'm all given out."

When Do I Get My Turn?

"All given out." What an interesting phrase. And not an unusual one. I see many women invest heavily in being great parents and wonderful wives. But all too often, after all those years of giving, nothing seems to be happening. Like Ruth, they reach their late thirties and begin to feel disappointed because all their sacrificial dedication doesn't seem to be paying off.

Ruth has worked hard to fulfill her expected role. She is still expected to give, give, give, and rarely receives a reward for her labor. After all, she has earned those rewards hundreds of times over, hasn't she? Ruth's cry is echoed by millions of unhappy women across the country: "Isn't it about time I got my turn?"

But it seems someone forgot to tell the kids, the husband, or the boss. "My husband is as demanding as ever," Ruth says, "but I hardly ever get to talk to him anymore. He's always working. Joe says it's to give us future security, but I wonder . . . is it possible he's seeing another woman?"

"It wouldn't be the first time," I said. "But that's a serious accusation. Can you back it up?"

"Not exactly, but I feel he's building an invisible wall. I've tried everything to get through—crying, pleading, ignoring him—but it's hopeless. My efforts are about as effective as trying to knock down a house with a Nerf ball. At times I wonder why I even bother, because he's acting like such a jerk."

"Perhaps he's going through a mid-life crisis," I suggested.

"Yes, and I must be understanding and forgiving, mustn't I?" Ruth said sarcastically. "Well, who's going to understand me? What about *my* needs?"

Ruth clasped and unclasped her hands, then continued. "Oh, and that's not all. My son Jeff—he's fourteen—told me the other day, 'I don't need you telling me what to do, Mom. I'm not a baby anymore. I can make my own decisions.' That night he *borrowed* our friend's motor home to run to the Mini-Mart, then proceeded to run it into a telephone pole. To top it off, my father had a heart attack and Mom needs my help to care for him. I keep telling myself, *You can make it, Ruth. Remember, you're a rock.* I'm a rock, all right—crumbly shale. And I feel like everyone is pulling me apart."

Ruth's situation isn't unusual. Often in mid-life, when a woman is struggling with her own role in life, everyone else is, too. Her children are often hitting a stormy adolescence, her parents are growing older and needing her care, and her husband is having his own brand of mid-life troubles.

Ruth feels she is receiving less and less respect and love. All these years of hoping and dreaming that someday her family would be at peace, her marriage deep and intimate, seems to have been for nothing.

One part of her wants to bail out. Yet deep down, in the middle of all the turmoil, she has optimism, feeling that somehow she will have the happiness she deserves. If she can just keep on keeping on, the Cinderella story, with its "happy ever after" ending, might someday be hers.

Welcome to the Mid-Life Malaise

As Ruth told me her story, I was tempted to say, "Welcome to the mid-life malaise." Entering the late thirties is a little like walking into the world beyond the looking glass in Lewis Carroll's *Alice: Through the Looking Glass.* Crazy things happen, and you don't know what will hit you next.

The word *malaise* means a sensation of discomfort, being uneasy or indisposed, a slowed-down, droopy feeling. I think that quite adequately describes a woman's world as she travels through mid-life.

How did Ruth and so many other women get to this crazy

place? Why is her once-happy marriage and life falling apart? There are probably a lot of reasons, and we certainly can't go into them all, but I do want to consider three possibilities.

First, there is the busyness. Too often we let the habit of being too busy become a thief who embezzles time from the development of relationships between husbands and wives. For many, the twenties and thirties was a time for working hard, beginning a family, and saving for a dream house. When problems would pop up, they would simply shove them in a closet with the intention of "talking later, when things quiet down and the kids are not around." But somehow they never got around to talking. Now they may find they hardly know each other and have little or nothing in common anymore.

Second, an unsatisfied relationship with husbands often brings on a "soul hunger"—a deep inner need for understanding and romance.

Third, because of this growing hunger, women often have unrealistic expectations of marriage and their husbands. Some husbands can't or won't try to understand or meet their wives' increasing needs at this time. They may be going through a tough mid-life transition, too.

Although it will eventually pass, mid-life, for both the husband and wife, can be a lean time, a hard time, and a barren time. Let's look at these endangered marriages in a bit more detail.

Fall-apart Marriages

One of the critical and probably the most distressing situation to come out of the male and female mid-life malaise is the fall-apart marriage. Marriage fatality is greater in this phase than any other. I have counseled literally hundreds of men and women who have divorced or seriously considered divorce during this time. I find however, that more women fantasize about divorce than follow through.

Many times a woman finds her marriage is turning stale, rancid, and dry as a midsummer day. The happiness of those first few blissful years may be as wilted and listless as unwatered petunias in a drought.

They never agree on anything anymore. If they aren't arguing about children, they fuss at each other over finances. She and her husband are spending less and less time together. Communication has become practically nonexistent. It doesn't seem fair; just when she needs him most, he's pulling away.

Such is the case with Sally, a beautifully groomed woman of 41. Sally sought my help for what she called a wretched marriage, yet she appeared to have a good deal that could make for happiness. She owned a fine home and drove an expensive-looking little sports car. Despite her obvious wealth, she suffered from depression and headaches.

When she told me about her past, she mentioned a very romantic artist she had once dated. "I can't seem to forget him," she said. "I didn't marry him at the time because he was very poor and I needed stability. Sometimes now I think I would rather live in a tent with a man who understands me than in this palace with a man who's hardly ever home."

Unfortunately Sally has reached a point in her life where she desperately needs more emotional nurturing than her husband can give her, so she's reaching into her past for someone to fill that need.

Sally imagines this artist could meet her inner needs and begins to fantasize how different her life could have been if she had married him. He becomes a sort of ghost lover who (at least in her dreams) can come to the rescue and meet her deepest needs. The artist's memory offers her an escape from unpleasant reality.

The need in Sally's life isn't necessarily sexual, although at times sex becomes a neglected part of a marriage when communication is failing. When a husband backs away, a wife may feel inadequate about her sexuality. But a woman needs more than sex. She needs a man to talk to her, listen to her, understand her, feed her soul hunger.

She might visualize a husband so in tune with her body and soul that he can anticipate and meet her every mood and desire. Ideally, he would be the cello, she the flute, and together their music would make a harmonious, joyous love song.

But too often their music is out of tune. He seems to hit all the wrong notes, and she keeps getting out of sync. When the tunes come out all wrong and she can't seem to get the songs right, what can she do? Where can she go? Who will meet her needs? There is a song deep inside her that must be sung—another part of her that must be played.

Are You in a Mid-Life Slump?

Do you relate to Ruth or Sally? Are you experiencing some of the difficulties they are in the middle years of your life?

Below you'll find a questionnaire developed to help women identify their symptoms and discover whether or not they are suffering from what I call the late thirties-early forties slump or malaise. Simply read each question and indicate your yes or no answer by placing an X in the appropriate space.

And please, be honest in your answers. I made the mistake once of giving the test to a group of women when their husbands were with them. Several women came up to me later and made comments such as, "Jean, I'm so sorry, but I wasn't being honest with all of my answers. I couldn't answer some of those questions with my husband sitting right beside me."

If you feel inhibited, go off by yourself. Write your answers on another paper and burn it when you're finished, to make certain no one but you and God know what you've admitted to.

	Yes	No
1. I have been experiencing a drop in my energy level.	__	__
2. On some days I get this draggy, listless, blah feeling.	__	__
3. I lack interest in sex.	__	__
4. My earlier interests or hobbies don't seem important anymore.	__	__
5. I'm experiencing boredom with activities and duties I once loved.	__	__
6. I'm having episodes of depression unrelated to my menstrual cycle.	__	__
7. Some days I get this feeling of foreboding.	__	__
8. I find myself overreacting and getting touchier over small irritations.	__	__
9. I have crying spells more frequently.	__	__
10. I get these "crazy days," when I feel I'm bursting apart.	__	__
11. I'm having more difficulty making decisions. I want others to decide for me.	__	__
12. I find myself having memory lapses. I can't recall where I put things, or a person's name.	__	__
13. I have increased feelings of failure.	__	__
14. I often feel unneeded or useless.	__	__
15. I don't think others love me as much now as in the past.	__	__

Yes No

16. Sometimes I get to wondering about my spiritual life. Am I really a Christian? Am I actually a bad person who's wearing a virtuous mask?   ___ ___

17. I have these dreams that someday my true love is going to come for me.   ___ ___

18. At times I have romantic notions or daydreams.   ___ ___

19. I often want to escape my present situation.   ___ ___

20. I read romantic novels or watch soap operas as a form of escape.   ___ ___

21. I think a lot about "if only's," or what I would do differently if I could live my life over again.   ___ ___

22. I often regret past decisions or choices.   ___ ___

23. I worry about past mistakes.   ___ ___

24. I spend a lot of time thinking of who I am and what I have become.   ___ ___

25. I often wonder if I am actually in early menopause.   ___ ___

If you were able to answer mostly no to these statements, chances are you are not into the mid-life phase or you have a mild case. However, if your yes's outnumbered the no's, you are probably going through or edging into what psychologists and society have termed a "mid-life crisis."

I really don't like the term "mid-life crisis." I'd choose a milder name, such as "late thirties/early forties slump or malaise." Perhaps it could even be called a "mid-life syndrome." *Crisis* indicates something terrible and irreversible has happened, and this malaise certainly isn't permanent or critical. In fact, there are new theories about this mid-life phenomenon. Some experts suggest it may actually be a period of adjustment—a kind of developmental stage, much like puberty—that we must pass through in order to get on with the next phase of our lives.

There may even be a medical reason for at least a part of the mid-life slump. Could all this craziness have something to do with our hormones?

Could It Be My Hormones? ──── ༅

To answer the question ending the last chapter, yes. Many of the symptoms seen in women suffering from the late thirties/early forties slump could be the result of subtle hormonal changes as their bodies prepare to go into premenopause.

I wouldn't suggest that all the symptoms seen in mid-life are premenopausal. On the other hand, I totally disagree with psychologists who blame the entire mid-life problem on the individual's mental health. Quite frankly, I think we're looking at a whole body process here: physical, psychological, emotional, cultural, and social. And it amounts to no small problem.

"She Used to Be So Friendly"

Several years ago, a man came to me seeking counsel over a concern about his wife. "She's become so tired and listless lately. It's like she's turning into an entirely different per-

son. I don't know what to think. My Rachael used to be so
friendly and outgoing. She used to be so happy. Now she's
depressed and discouraged and nothing I do seems to lift
her spirits. She's only forty-one and drags around as if she
were eighty. She went in for a complete physical, and the
doctor said she was in perfect health and suggested she
might just need a vacation. I know it's more than that. I was
hoping maybe you could suggest something."

"Can you give me an example of something she's said or
done recently that would help me see the problem more
clearly?" I asked.

"Yes. There was one incident a couple of weeks ago. Actually that's what really convinced me I needed to get professional help. We were at her family's annual picnic. Her
relatives have this big bash every year, with family coming
in from all over the country. Rachael has always looked
forward to this time of being with her brothers and sisters.
This time, Rachael was talking to her sister. They had a
minor disagreement and Rachael literally blew up. She
spoiled the picnic for everyone."

"Has she ever done anything like this before?"

"Never," he said. "Her behavior was extremely out of
character, overreactive, and completely unnecessary. Since
then she's gotten worse—often touchy, easily irritated, and
she cries a lot. Oh, and another thing, she's almost completely lost interest in her recipe collection. She's always
loved international cooking and has collected recipes from
famous chefs all over the world. Now she complains
through mealtimes about how she hates to cook, and I find
myself taking her out more and more to avoid the hassles."

When I talked with Rachael, she related the same story,
adding that she often had the "blahs"—days when she
didn't feel like doing much of anything. She also complained of depression, when all she wanted to do was stay
in bed and sleep.

I saw Rachael and her husband in the early years of my practice. Since then, I have seen her symptoms over and over again in women between the ages of thirty-five and forty-five.

Let's have a closer look at the most prevalent symptoms of this mid-life slump:

Drop in energy levels   Many women complain of "blah" days, with mild depression that makes them feel listless, lethargic, or draggy.

Decreased interest in sex   This has been a concern for some women at this time, particularly as women in their mid-thirties and forties normally experience a sexual peak.

Morbidness or sadness   Comes on for no particular reason. Often women will complain of unusual feelings of sorrow or that nothing is important to them anymore.

Loss of interest in hobbies or activities   Women like Rachael frequently lose interest or become bored with activities that once gave them great pleasure. One woman, who had always prided herself on her immaculate home, suddenly became very bored with it, and turned into a total slob.

Depression   This is probably the most prevalent symptom expressed by women in a late-thirties/early forties malaise.

Doldrums   Many women complain about a foreboding feeling that something unpleasant is about to happen.

Touchiness and overreactiveness   This is one of the most common complaints, even in women who usually describe themselves as happy and easygoing.

Crying spells   Often occur in women at this time.

Crazy days These can be a frightening phenomenon. Women suffering from the mid-life slump often complain of days when everything goes wrong and they feel almost out of control.

Increasing dependency Frequently seen as women avoid making decisions and want others to decide for them. For example, difficulty in deciding which restaurant to eat at and what to order.

Memory lapses Common in women at this time. I was always forgetting names or places. I'd be heading for a certain room, and by the time I got there, I would forget why I'd gone.

Feeling unneeded or useless This feeling often accompanies the emptying nest as the children grow more independent and leave home.

Feeling unloved A common complaint among women whose husbands are heavily involved with their work. Many men are into their own mid-life transition at this time, and as Dr. Daniel Levinson says in his book *The Seasons of a Man's Life*, "Some men feel driven to break up the strangle hold of a well-ordered life." Men, too, are looking to escape, and quite often the woman's feelings of being unloved are valid.

Romantic notions or daydreams As I explained in the last chapter, these are commonly used by women experiencing problems during mid-life as a diversion or escape mechanism. Along with that, there is a distant hope and dream that true love and happiness lie just around the corner.

Wanting to escape   This is quite common, also. There is a desire to go somewhere away from the family, away from the problems.

Recapitulation   A troublesome phase appearing in some women. This simply means to review or sum up certain events of the past and express regret or worry over past decisions or mistakes. These women chastise themselves by hashing over things they did in the past that they might do differently now. Of course it's impossible to change history, but they will often make statements like, "How stupid of me to have let my daughter marry that boy. I should have known he'd bring nothing but trouble."

"If only I'd been able to see how incompatible my husband and I are. I never should have married him." Recapitulation is full of futile "if only's."

Introspection   Goes hand in hand with recapitulation. It means "looking inward as into one's own mind . . . self-examination." It is a "Woe is me" or "What's the use?" syndrome, where there is a lot of morbid preoccupation with the problems of the past, present, and future. Introspection often results in feelings of failure and a drastic drop in self-esteem.

Early menopause?   A great many women who are experiencing symptoms like these wonder about menopause. A woman in the slump will go to her doctor for a checkup. The doctor will likely say, "You're in perfect health, and no, it's too early for you to be in premenopause. You can expect to go another ten years before that happens." Perhaps he will pat you on the head and say, "It's just a phase you're going through." Or perhaps he will be sympathetic with all your emotional ups and downs and prescribe an antide-

pressant or suggest a few sessions with a good family therapist.

While the doctor could be right, he or she may be missing
an important element. I want to be very clear here: There is
no documented medical proof linking hormones to this
mid-life slump. But there have been some medical-journal
articles suggesting that such a link does exist.

I have read data from medical journals regarding the
slow, subtle hormone changes taking place in a woman's
body from the age of thirty-five on. One gynecologist with
whom I've consulted in this matter says this:

> This phase may be some years away from the menopause,
> yet it is one of the steps toward it. The ovaries are slowly
> becoming sluggish in their hormone production. The brain
> begins to pressure the ovaries by saying, "Hurry up, there.
> You must do your job better than this. I'll help." The ovary
> then receives a jolt of stimulus, which makes it work better
> for a while. Then soon the ovary starts getting lazy again. As
> the ovaries slowly slack off on the amount of estrogen they
> produce, the body is learning to adjust. It must learn to cope
> with lower estrogen levels in the bloodstream and bring in
> estrogen from other sources. This "forties slump" can be
> short-term or last up to two to five years.

Several years ago, I began sending some of the women I
saw in my practice to a local gynecologist and endocrine
specialist. These women suffered terribly from symptoms
of the late thirties/early forties slump. I knew this doctor
had been doing a lot of research in the area of women's
hormones. He used hormone therapy on selected patients
who exhibited debilitating symptoms. In most cases these
women reported positive results. I'd like to point out, however, that it is rare that a woman's symptoms will be severe
enough to require hormonal therapy during this phase.

Perimenopause and the Mid-Life Slump

For clarity, I'd like to take just a moment to review the reproductive life of women during our estrogen years. There are generally five stages throughout life showing the rise and fall of estrogen production from our ovaries.

Premenarche   Means prior to puberty, referring to our developmental years.

Menarche   Meaning the first period, the beginning of menses. It refers to one specific point in time.

Menstrual   Covers all our years of ovulating and menstruating and actually includes three phases:
- *Postmenarche*, which refers to those early menstrual years when irregularity is common.
- *Menstrual*, which covers those years of regular cycles, generally referring to women aged twenty to forty.
- *Perimenopause*, the time around menopause. It signifies a transition time, when cycles may vary slightly and symptoms of declining estrogen may appear. Perimenopause includes the *premenopause*, which is the time prior to the menopause when symptoms are obvious. The lay term for the entire process is the *climacteric*, or change of life.

Menopause   Signals the end of menstruation. It is a single point in time, but is often used more loosely to include the range of time when definite symptoms of estrogen deficiency—such as hot flashes and obvious changes in ovulation and menses—are present.

Postmenopause   Covers the years after menstruation has completely stopped.[1]

The mid-life slump seems to take place in the very early stages of perimenopause, before premenopause is actually diagnosed.

G. Virginia Upton, Ph.D., says in her article "The Perimenopause," "The symptoms experienced during the perimenopause can be quite indefinite. Fatigue, insomnia, depression and nervousness are common complaints." These she indicates are often attributed to the "vicissitudes of life."

Yet there is, as she relates in this article, "an almost imperceptible estrogen and progesterone decline accompanied by many apparently innocuous symptoms. . . ."

She also states that women go through two major menstrual transitions in life: adolescence and mid-life. "Changes occurring in adolescence during the postmenarchal years are much the same as those experienced by the woman over 40. The mood swings, the interrupted sleep patterns, etc., are subtle signs of change."[2]

Again I must state that there is no proof that the emotional turmoil experienced by women in their late thirties and early forties is hormonal. Unless a woman is actually showing physical signs of estrogen deficiency such as hot flashes and erratic bleeding, a doctor generally isn't going to treat her with hormone replacements. In fact, medical help in any form may be hard to come by and even unwise.

Perhaps you're wondering why I'd even bring up the possibility of the problem being hormonal if there is no medical help. I do so simply because it often helps to know what you're dealing with.

Another Possibility

I would be remiss in giving you information on the possibility of hormone involvement during mid-life if I only talked about perimenopause. There is another possibility, also hormonal. A woman suffering these symptoms could very well be experiencing PMS, not entering the climacteric phase.

According to Dr. Neils H. Lauersen, author of *Premenstrual Syndrome and You,* "Many women who experience menstrual irregularity, depression and weight gain in their forties immediately assume that because they feel different they are in menopause. Usually these women are not premenopausal (or perimenopausal) but are suffering varying degrees of premenstrual syndrome."

He goes on to say, "When a woman in her forties has gained weight, has lived through a stressful period, or has undergone tubal sterilization, she is a more likely candidate for PMS than for menopause."[3]

It is important to note this possibility because the hormone treatment for PMS is entirely different than that for menopause. PMS sufferers, when hormone therapy is prescribed, use a natural progesterone. Menopausal symptoms, however, require the use of estrogen.

Regardless of whether the hormonal fluctuations are PMS or perimenopausal, there is an end in sight to the misery.

Things Will Get Better

When talking with women who find themselves experiencing these symptoms, this question invariably comes up: "How long will I have to put up with this?"

In my observations, the perimenopausal slump hits somewhere between thirty-five and forty-five and will soon pass. I know that sounds a bit trite, but it's true.

The mid-life slump may be a time of uneven or unstable hormone production, which I for one believe produces many of those strange emotional reactions in us. With our hormones changing, even in a slow and subtle manner, it's no wonder we experience occasional panic or anxiety attacks. The emotions are often fleeting and sometimes come and go so fast we're left wondering what really happened.

I often liken this phase of fluctuating emotions to flying in a jumbo jet. Say we're cruising along above the clouds. The wind and rain hitting the ground can't touch us in this lofty, serene place. But suddenly the pilot turns on the Fasten Seat Belt signs and announces that we're heading into some turbulence.

Suddenly our smooth, high-flying airship starts heaving about like a carnival ride, and the serenity of moments before (for me, at least) turns to panic.

In situations like this I find it extremely difficult to concentrate on reading, sleeping, or eating. I pray the jet will be strong enough to overcome the prevailing winds. I'm fairly sure the plane will make it through, but what if . . .?

Since I'm a nervous traveler, I'd be compelled to ask the flight attendant something like, "Is everything okay with the plane? It's terribly bumpy."

"Oh, yes," would be her calm reply. "This is only a mild turbulence, and we'll be through it as soon as we cross over the mountain range."

Even though the jet is still bouncing, I always feel more comfortable knowing it will survive the buffeting wind and the uncomfortable part of the journey will soon be over.

I receive phone calls almost daily from women going through a rather bumpy ride as they experience the symptoms I've outlined in the last two chapters.

They almost always tell me, "I think I'm coming apart at the seams," or, "I get these crazy days when I feel like I'm going out of my mind."

They are experiencing turbulence and wondering if their ship will survive the storm. As a sort of "flight attendant" for women, I reassure them that they needn't worry. Most of us are proceeding directly on our journey through life and will arrive at our destination right on schedule. It is unfortunate that we have to go through fears and pain before we get there, but be assured, we will get there.

12

Managing
Mid-Life Malaise ⎯ ✤

We've talked about some of the problems women in their middle years often find themselves facing. In this chapter we'll be covering ways to manage this turbulent phase of life. My first management suggestion (and I'm sure this won't surprise you) is to see your doctor.

Get a Checkup

I would encourage all of you who are nearing your forties to make an appointment with a gynecologist for a complete physical. Your exam should include a manual breast exam, a mammogram (special X rays of the breasts), a pelvic exam with Pap smear, and perhaps even a cervical biopsy.

As much as possible, make certain all systems are healthy before you start a management regimen of your own. Discuss the suggestions I've outlined below with your doctor, especially if you have dietary or physical restrictions.

Diet Overhaul

In the late thirties and early forties it is not unusual to start having weight problems. How easy it is to pack on the pounds! It's as though our metabolism shifts into low gear and anything more caloric than a raw spinach leaf turns to fat the minute we look at it.

Most American women are constantly dieting, skipping meals, and cutting calories. We lose an average of 200 pounds a year each. The problem is, the pounds rarely stay off.

There are dozens of fad diets on the market guaranteed to take weight off. What they don't tell us is that they are also guaranteed to put the weight back on the minute we stop the diet. Many of these diets are lacking in the vital nutrients we need to stay healthy.

Doctors are constantly after us to avoid fads. They tell us not to skip meals, to eat foods low in fats and complex carbohydrates with high fiber. Their concern isn't only for our figures, but also our health. It is a known fact that obesity increases the risk of heart attack, coronary artery disease, atherosclerosis, diabetes, and cancer.

An article I read in *The Journal of Reproductive Medicine* said this: "Countries that have high incidence of breast cancer are usually those with higher standards of living and whose diets include greater dietary fat and caloric intake." The article goes on to say, "the incidence of breast cancer in these affluent populations also increases with age. In contrast, low risk countries show exactly opposite trends." The article gives the following example: "Breast cancer in American women is six times that of Japanese women; Americans consume 300 percent more fat than do the Japanese."[1]

We can't go wrong if we stay with the basic food groups,

keep our calorie intake at a safe minimum level, and maintain a healthy level of activity to burn those calories.

In addition to a nutritious diet, you may want to ask your doctor about taking supplemental vitamins and minerals. Many doctors recommend that women begin taking calcium tablets at this time to guard against osteoporosis in postmenopausal years.

Exercise

How many times have you heard it: Eat sensibly and develop an exercise plan. Well, I'm going to mention it again. Exercise makes an enormous difference in keeping weight under control. It also helps to reduce tension, which is especially helpful during these stress-filled years.

Since many of us have jobs and responsibilities that require little actual physical endurance, some form of regular exercise has almost become a necessity in order to assure fitness.

Reducing Tension

Because the mid-life transition is a high-anxiety time of life, we need to spend some time developing tension reducing skills. I gave some suggestions on reducing tension in chapter nine, but I'd like to add a few more to the list.

First of all, we need to understand how tension works. To help you better understand, I've devised a tension formula: Negative stimuli build up > frustration > anger > tension > discharge >>>.

All tension will eventually discharge. For some it comes out in arguments, for others through psychosomatic illness such as headaches, backaches, ulcers, colitis, and so forth. The trick is to deal quickly with the negative stimuli, frustration, anger, and tension before they discharge in a way that can hurt relationships and your body. Left to build, tension can do great damage to us, as well as to others. Fortunately, we can discharge that built-up tension in several healthy, acceptable ways.

Release it to the Lord   The first step is to learn to recognize a negative stimulus and deal with the problem before it deals with you. One very effective way to handle a tension-building situation is to release it to the Lord.

Many years ago, my very close friend Mary and I were heading up an important project for the church. I didn't think anything could ever come between us; I was wrong.

One day my friend repeated some potentially damaging criticism she'd heard about my husband's business. I was furious. Of course I knew it couldn't be true. I was not only angry that she'd repeat gossip, but that she'd believe it. I'd received a lethal dose of negative stimuli, and it almost ruined our friendship.

Rather than confront her and straighten the matter out immediately, I fretted and stewed for days. My fury grew until I became tense and angry with everyone. I began plotting my revenge, but the idea of revenge went against my Christian values.

One part of me seemed to be saying, "Hurt her. She deserves to be punished for what she did."

Another part argued, "No, that isn't right. Open your Bible and see what God wants you to do about your anger toward her."

Thankfully, after struggling with these opposing thoughts, I obeyed the second voice. I opened my Bible to Psalm 37, simply because I remembered that Psalm had been of great help to me before. As I read it, I knew I'd made the right choice.

"Commit your way to the Lord; trust in him; and he will act. . . . Be still before the Lord and wait patiently for him. . . . Refrain from anger, and forsake wrath! Fret not yourself; it tends only to evil" (vv. 5, 7, 8 RSV).

From there, my study lead me to Romans 12:17–19, 21. "Repay no one evil for evil but take thought for what is noble in the sight of all. If possible, so far as it depends upon you, live peaceably with all. Beloved never avenge yourselves, but leave it to the wrath of God; for it is written, 'Vengeance is mine, I will repay, says the Lord.' . . . Do not be overcome by evil, but overcome evil with good" (RSV).

I could tell the Lord was, in a real sense, standing me in the corner. He showed me yet another verse that pointed out how wrong my held-in anger and thoughts of revenge were. Hebrews 12:15 said, "See to it that no one fail to obtain the grace of God; that no 'root of bitterness' spring up and cause trouble, and by it the many become defiled" (RSV).

It wasn't easy, but I dropped to my knees and prayed, "O Lord, I have been angry and tense for three days. I can't handle these feelings or make them go away. Yet Your Word says I can't hit back and that You'll handle it for me. You say I am to wait patiently, to trust and rest in You. I know I must relinquish the whole matter to You forever. I will wait, but I'm still furious; what am I to do with these feelings? If I'm not supposed to feel anger, then please take it away."

I felt I'd been in God's presence and that He would somehow take care of the matter. Without even trying, I soon realized I was thinking about my friend's betrayal less and less. A few days later she came to me begging forgiveness, having discovered her information had been false.

I found myself saying, "Of course I forgive you. I knew it was all a mistake, and there's no need to discuss it further." God had completely removed my anger, bitterness, and built-up tension. But had I not turned the matter over to God, I might have acted out, discharged that tension, and lost a dear friend.

To confront or not to confront   Some therapists will recommend direct and immediate confrontation as a means of putting a stop to tension-building problems. I tend to disagree with this method.

I don't think it's generally wise to confront someone in the first flush of anger. In order to confront without hurting a relationship, we need more understanding and information about the problem. We need a cooling down period to avoid damaging relationships even more.

One time my mother wrote me a critical, unkind letter about the behavior of my children. It hurt terribly, as I felt I could never measure up to what she expected. My first response was anger. I wrote her a defensive, nasty letter.

I never mailed it, though, because I got this overwhelming feeling, which I knew was from God, to tear it up. I'm glad I did, because two weeks later my mother was hospitalized with heart trouble.

Later she said to me, "Can you forget that letter? I was so depressed when I wrote it, and I never meant what I said. You've always been the strong one, and I'm afraid I dumped my frustrations on you."

Sometimes confrontation is the answer, but be sure to count the cost. Consider first what your response will do to the person and the relationship.

Debriefing tension   Aside from waiting for God to help, there are some healthy ways we can debrief our tension. I like the word *debriefing* in this sense. Debriefing is a quiet, deliberate activity that drains the tension from us and at the same time revitalizes us.

There are a number of ways we can debrief. First, we can talk about the issue with a trusted friend and confidant. Often by the time you've talked it out, you have control of your feelings and can more easily find a solution. After a debriefing session you may feel more in control, more able to face the problem.

But sometimes a person may inflict a wound so deep that we simply can't talk to anyone for a while, or perhaps the problem is too intimate. Another debriefing method is to write out your feelings, frustrations, and anger on paper. Journalizing can be a resourceful and therapeutic tool in working out tension.

Other tension debriefers include: time alone; leisurely shopping; quiet walks; creative work or hobbies such as painting, sculpting, knitting, sewing, and so on.

Also, try talking to God. He is the one friend and confidant you can always trust. He will never betray you, and He always understands. I especially love debriefing with God, because He will either give me an answer, give me strength to move on, or He will ease away the tension and give me peace. Sometimes I get all three.

Along with debriefing comes a more physical way of dealing with tension.

Defusing tension   Defusing tension is another method I find useful in expelling or pushing tensions out of my life. It differs subtly from debriefing in that debriefing is a sort of draining off of tension. Defusing is literally keeping a bomb from exploding, or quenching a fire before it burns out of control. Defusing requires a quick release of energy.

You can defuse tension by weeding the garden, running, swimming, or doing any intense activity that leaves you physically tired.

I have often been asked how I survived all those years of

counseling, listening to, and bearing the burdens of so many hurting people. There are two answers. First, the Lord strengthens me daily because I'm doing what He has called me to do. Second, I have a lot of interests to help debrief and defuse tension. I've always loved antiques, and for the last few years I've been involved in creating an authentic Somerset cottage complete with an English country garden.

Feeding Soul Hunger

Many women in their thirties and forties have unfulfilled needs in the area of romance, love, attention, and understanding. What does a woman do when her husband can't or won't meet those needs? What can a woman do to fill the emptiness inside, which at times almost seems to consume her? What does a woman do with a husband who doesn't bring her flowers anymore? Divorce him? Have an affair?

Heaven forbid! Most women would rather not opt for either, but they would love to turn their husbands into a new man. I often hear women saying, "If only my husband could meet my needs. If only he could understand me."

All right, suppose we explore the option of changing your man a bit further. Is it possible to change a man's tune to match a woman's? Will his melody and hers ever blend?

Why Can't a Man Be More Like a Woman?

While we may be able to do a little in tuning up a man, my experience clearly shows we'd better not count on that change. Men will never truly be able to understand women or to meet their needs, simply because they are *not* women.

Remember Rex Harrison and the role he played in *My Fair Lady*? At one point in the movie, when he was totally exasperated by Eliza's tearful display of emotions, he sang, "Why Can't a Woman Be More Like a Man?" The truth of it is, he couldn't understand her moods and wanted to change her so *he* wouldn't feel so inadequate. But a woman can't be like a man, any more than a man can be like a woman. We are different.

Women are romantic creatures by nature, and most men, with their analytical way of thinking, seldom if ever can meet all of a woman's needs.

Forty-two-year-old Sandra complained that her husband was so busy with his work that he never paid any attention to her. "I want to talk to him about my feelings and frustrations, and I want him to do the same. He just rejects me and seems to prefer holding everything inside. He never confides in me. We've been married for ten years, but I'm so unhappy I don't know if I can go on. I feel like I'm starving emotionally. I don't want a divorce, but I don't know what else to do."

"Perhaps your husband isn't rejecting you," I suggested. "Suppose he simply isn't capable of meeting your romantic demands?"

"Then maybe I'll just have to get a divorce."

"Do you really think divorce is the answer?" I asked.

"Oh, I don't know. I have to do something. I can't go on like this."

Then I said, "What would you do if your husband had a serious accident and his injury left him partially paralyzed? Would you leave him?"

"Of course not. I would give him all the support and help he needed to get well again."

"But that doesn't fit with what you said earlier about being at the end of your patience. You indicated that if your husband couldn't meet your needs you would have to get a divorce."

"Well, that's different. If he were injured, he couldn't possibly meet my needs. I wouldn't expect that of him."

"Have you ever thought your husband might possibly be handicapped right now?"

"What do you mean?" she asked.

"Some men are emotionally handicapped when it comes to meeting a woman's needs. Your husband simply may not know how, and your pressure frightens him and keeps him from even trying."

"Oh, I see what you mean. If that's really the case, maybe I should give it another try."

Sandra did try, and although it hasn't been easy, Sandra says their marriage is recovering nicely.

I've counseled men who have had a difficult time with close relationships. Some have shared with me that getting too close emotionally makes them feel vulnerable. Others feel that being a strong leader means preserving some distance in order to maintain respect.

In my own family, my husband has at times hidden serious worries from me and been rather remote because he felt it was his duty to protect me from his burdens.

As difficult a pill as it may be to swallow, most men simply aren't able to meet all of a woman's needs. In fact, one man, whose wife became quite demanding about it, said, "No, I can't meet her needs, and frankly, I don't want to."

That man was going through his own mid-life transition and acted out his frustrations by leaving his wife for another woman. I don't condone this sort of action, but in this man's case, I certainly understand why he left. His wife was placing too many demands on him, and he simply didn't have the capacity to meet them.

I'm not saying that husbands have no responsibility here or that it is a woman's fault when a man walks out. It's often the other way around. I am simply suggesting that women not expect too much from their men, lest they push them into making that final decision to end the marriage. I've seen it happen many, many times.

I don't think we can count on changing our men significantly, so suppose we explore another avenue to satisfy our soul hunger.

Ghost Lovers and Other Fantasies

I first came across the phrase *soul hunger* in one of Eleanor Roosevelt's diaries. She had a very disappointing life in the early years of her marriage and longed for a deeper relationship with her husband. At one point she wrote, "How will my soul hunger ever be met?" That really started me thinking.

As I began to mull over these needs so prevalent in women, I decided to do some checking. I learned a few interesting facts. Women today, literally, are reading millions of romantic novels every month. That's right, *every month*.

Cynthia, a 42-year-old Christian woman, recently admitted to reading romances.

"Why do you read romances?" I asked.

"They provide a means of escape. Besides, I enjoy them. They are a kind of diversion for me. When stresses build up, I can run a steamy bubble bath, grab a good novel off the shelf, and mindlessly escape into another world."

Cynthia represents scores of women in their thirties and forties. As I talked with her in more detail, she confessed that she longs for a deeper understanding of her emotional needs and that there is a sort of loneliness in the form of soul hunger gnawing at her insides. She longs for her mate to be more romantic and understanding.

"I know I could never have an affair," Cynthia told me.

"That would be wrong. So I read romances. Some of the other gals I talk to watch the soaps instead. I'd rather read, but it all accomplishes the same end. For me, books seem to fill at least part of the void in my life."

"Do you have any other means of escape, aside from the books, I mean? I've talked with a good many women who talk of fantasizing during this time. They dream up what I call a ghost lover. What do you think about that?"

"Yeah, I can relate to that," she laughed. "When my husband, Ken, would rather be with his business than me, or when he just plain ignores my needs, I invent a sort of ghost lover."

When I asked her to explain what this phantom was like, she said:

> He's a cross between Paul Newman and Robert Redford. In my daydreams, he worships me and brings me flowers. Ken never brings me flowers. My ghost lover understands my every thought and fulfills all my desires.
>
> Well, for example, the other morning my husband and I were getting dressed. I moaned and said, "Oh, I do wish I could lose a few pounds. Sometimes all this dieting seems so useless."
>
> Ken frowned and yanked on his socks. "For heaven's sake, Cynthia, I'm tired of hearing about your weight. Either lose it or shut up about it."
>
> My ghost lover would never have been so harsh. He would have taken me in his arms and sighed, "Darling, it overwhelms me to think of how hard you struggle to please me. I'd love to see you meet your goal. But believe me, I love you just the way you are." He would have understood my need to be consoled, not scolded. My ghost lover builds up my shattered ego and feeds my soul.

The Pitfalls of Daydreams

But even as she spoke, I recognized a possible pitfall in Cynthia's daydreams. "Aren't you afraid this ghost lover of yours will lead you to expect too much of your husband?" I asked. "I know human nature, and if you put too much stock in these fantasy heroes on stage and in books, it could hurt your marriage," I added.

"I see what you mean," replied Cynthia. "But no, I'm fully aware that there really are no Prince Charmings in the world. I think I have a healthy hold on reality. It's just that I can't deny my thoughts and feelings. They are part of reality, too. I just need some way to deal with them, so I don't act out by actually running off with some guy and having an affair. I use my romance novels and my ghost lover as a diversion when my real world hurts too much to stay real."

Cynthia and other women may believe that romance novels and ghost lovers are therapeutic for those times when they feel the need for a little romance in their lives. My caution, however, would be for them to frequently evaluate themselves. Consider, for example, these questions:

Yes No

1. Are you spending more time escaping reality than dealing with it? ___ ___

2. Are you wishing more and more you could find someone who really cares? ___ ___

3. Are you dwelling more on your husband's faults than on his good points? ___ ___

4. Do you often neglect your duties so you can slip into the fantasy world of romance? ___ ___

5. Do you resent or become angry about occasional interruptions from your children or husband while you are escaping? ___ ___

Yes No

6. Are you reading more than one novel a day
or spending more than four hours a day in your
romantic diversion?   __ __

If you have answered yes to any of these questions, then
perhaps you need to step back and consider your motives.
While reading romances and entertaining ghost lovers may
provide a harmless diversion occasionally, there are other,
perhaps more constructive, ways to feed your soul hunger
and at the same time strengthen and improve your marriage.

Work on Relationships

Sometimes your soul hunger can be filled by concentrating at least some of your energy on your relationships. If
you are married, you may want to consider trying to revive
your wilting marriage.

Have an affair with your husband Surprise him with a
trip to the islands. If your budget can't stand the strain, take
a weekend and go to the beach or to a lovely resort—without the kids. Splurge a little. Treat him as if he were the
hero of your latest romantic novel. Yes, it's wild and zany,
and it may not work. But it just might be a start to a new
and exciting relationship.

Ask God to heal your marriage Ask Him to instill in you a
deep, unconditional love for your mate. Laura, a woman of
42, found she'd come to almost hate her husband at times.
She thought more and more about divorce.

"I knew it was wrong, the way I felt about him," she said.
"So I prayed that God would give me the kind of love for
my husband that He had. I am still in awe over the results of

that prayer. God helped me see I had been focusing on all the negative aspects of my husband and our marriage. I began to mentally take note of all the things that were good," she continued, "and found myself thinking more and more about those positive traits in him. Now, although our marriage is not a storybook affair, it's working. I do find, though, that I have to repeat my prayer on a regular basis."

Consider an accredited marriage counselor Find one whose goal is to help you pull together.

Make an effort to learn all you can about your husband In time, he may become your best friend.

Turn Toward God

When your diversions are an empty cup and your attempts to revitalize your marriage seem all for nothing, you may want to consider turning toward God. Spend time in prayer. Ask God to redirect your path. Use the Bible and other study books as your diversion for a time. Try falling in love with the Lord. I met a woman recently who had done just that.

Emily told me she had gotten hooked on romances. She was reading one to two a day.

> I'd get annoyed if anyone wanted anything, even a meal. My husband began looking more and more like the villain instead of the hero, and it got to where I could hardly stand to be around him. I realized I'd gotten in over my head and decided to quit. That wasn't easy. In fact, for a while I got worse. I started reading them on the sly. I'd given up reading everything except those romances—including my Bible.

I forced myself to go back to spending a few minutes in the Bible every day and spent a lot of time in prayer, asking God to help me do the right thing. I asked Him to put a hunger in my heart for Him instead of for romance. He did. I still read an occasional romance, but now I'm careful to keep praying that God will be first in my life. With God, I don't need a ghost lover or a Prince Charming. Actually, I don't really need those romances anymore, but I love to read, and sometimes I'll read a romantic novel. But now I do it for enjoyment, not to fill a deep romantic need.

Perhaps Emily has indeed found the answer to fill her soul hunger. You may want to try it.

Set aside a time each day for prayer and study of God's Word. Ask God to feed your soul hunger. Tell Him you'd like to hunger and thirst after Him, not fantasy lovers. Relax and let God change you from the inside.

As God redirects your life—and believe me, if you're sincere, He will—you'll want to think about new and challenging ways to fill your days.

Plan New Goals

There's nothing like a new set of goals to freshen your mind and your outlook on life.

Along with mid-life comes the need to look over your life. You'll naturally observe where you've been and what you've accomplished over the last few years. For many women, this is the time to reevaluate their lives, to reset their priorities and think about what they really want to accomplish during the rest of their lives.

Over and over again in my years as a counselor, I saw women who had put their own lives on hold while they cared for and reared a family. Don't get me wrong; I think this is a highly admirable trait. But many of these women come into their forties depressed, discouraged, and (some of them) divorced. They had such high hopes and expectations. They knew they'd made the right choice in the beginning, but what happened? Why does a woman reach forty and suddenly feel as if she's failed?

Too many women forget to take into account that their initial decision—to stay home with the kids or to embark on a career—isn't necessarily a lifetime one. We must always be ready and willing to learn, grow, and change. We will do well to develop our own special talents, no matter what other tasks we must do.

I have lost count of the number of husbands who tell me their wives have become boring. I've seen women turn stale and stagnant because they get set in a certain life-style and are afraid to move out of it. The pattern becomes a sort of comfort zone, and even though it has problems, at least they are familiar problems.

This can be dangerous to the woman and to her marriage. Often men in this age group are restless, dreaming of new challenges and change. Wives can't afford the luxury of staying in their mental comfort zone, because too often it leads to mental stagnation.

Each of us was created with specific and unique talents and abilities. Unless we develop those talents and use them throughout our lives, we stand a good chance of growing stale and uninteresting to ourselves and to others.

Abraham Maslow, the famous psychologist, made this statement: "Every human must find his God-given mission in this life and in the search, therein, lies his identity."

Even in this modern society, where women have been encouraged to do their own thing and find fulfillment, there are still many women who have been so busy with others they've not taken the time to be themselves. Also, many women who thought they were doing their own thing years ago now look at their lives and realize they made a mistake. Others may have made the right choice and been fulfilling their God-given task, but now feel restless and dissatisfied. Restlessness in mid-life is often God's hand at your back, urging you to move on, to reevaluate and perhaps alter your course.

Many women come to this point in time with a yearning that can't be filled. Over and over I hear women complain that they'd like more out of life. One might say, "If only I'd finished college. I wanted so much to be a teacher. I quit school to get married and have a family. Now it's too late." Another might lament, "I'm so lonely now that my children are off to college. I can't bear this empty house."

No matter what the lament, there is an answer. For a woman who wants a career—go back to school. For a woman whose home has become an empty nest—find ways to fill those days with work, hobbies, volunteer work, women's groups, foster children, or other useful activities. The point is, we can *do* something about that emptiness.

Whether we work at home or outside the home, it is important we seek our special mission and get our lives on the right track. When we are excited about our God-given mission or task, we become encouraged about life. We are not only more interesting to ourselves, we stimulate and encourage others. And that can go a long way in making the miserable symptoms of the mid-life malaise easier to handle.

A woman may need to grow for the sake of making herself more interesting to her man, but much more importantly, she must keep growing and learning for herself. As you learn and grow, keep praying this prayer:

"I am a special, unique person in Your eyes, God. No one else in all the universe is in my place, nor could anyone actually take my place. And I thank You for loving me. God, what do You want me to do with the rest of my life? What is Your mission for me?"

A Woman
of Mystique   ჰ

On June 3, 1937, King Edward VIII gave up the throne of England to marry the woman he loved. In a moving broadcast that shook the world, he had declared, "I have found it impossible to carry the heavy burden of responsibility and to discharge my duties as king, as I wish to do, without the help and support of the woman I love."

The romance between King Edward VIII and Mrs. Wallis Simpson became a legend—the love story of the century. The greatness of his love for her created a political crisis in England.

How many men today would abdicate a throne for the love of a woman? I doubt many would. What kind of woman would it take to make a man walk away forever from all that money, position, authority, and security? It would take a woman of mystique, a quality I find sorely lacking in women today.

Men are still abdicating their kingdoms for women. The problem is, their kingdoms often consist of a home, a wife, children, and a job. My case loads have been full of women whose husbands have given up everything and gone off with another woman. After ten, fifteen, even twenty years of marriage, the man suddenly wants out. He's ready for new blood, adventure, a woman who's alluring, charming, and different.

Why Do Husbands Leave?

I've heard the sad tale time and time again; the storybook marriage ends up with the last few pages missing. The husband, originally a prince, turns into a real toad. Shortly thereafter, hubby pulls his character out of the script and disappears into another woman's story, appearing there, of course, as Prince Charming.

Why do husbands take mistresses or walk out on their wives? There are many reasons, and perhaps the wife has done nothing to cause his wanderings. But sometimes, more often than I like to think, the husband leaves because he feels he needs a change. Many men have told me they find their wives boring. "If I want to talk about my job, politics, sports, or world affairs, I have to do it with other people," one of these men told me. "My wife simply is not informed about the things that interest me."

Another man agreed with me that he had a marvelous wife. She was a good mother and wife, and supportive of him. Yet this man had taken a mistress. This was an extremely difficult case for me. I almost found myself hating this man for his insensitivity and shallow thinking. But he said some things that made me want to find out why a man would do this sort of thing. "My wife is one of the best women I know," he said to me. "But my mistress—well, she turns on my mind."

He agreed he'd never be able to find another woman as good as his wife, but she had made one grave mistake:

She'd become satisfied with her role as wife and mother and simply stopped growing as a person.

There is yet another serious mistake wives often make—losing their self-respect—which Dr. James Dobson discusses in his book *Love Must Be Tough*.

To illustrate, Henry and Marsha's marriage of twenty years is falling apart. Henry is less interested in the relationship than Marsha. She's put her whole life into this marriage and isn't about to let go.

Henry has been spending more and more time away from home. Marsha seems to be doing more and more complaining about it. One day Henry announces he's leaving. Feeling horrified and rejected, Marsha throws herself at his feet, begging, "Please don't leave me, Henry. We need you. I need you, the children need you. I'll do anything you say; just please don't go."

As a final act of desperation, she grabs his leg and lets herself be dragged across the floor as Henry grabs his bag and heads for the door. He shakes her loose in the entryway and, with a look of disgust, walks out, slamming the door behind him.

Marsha lost all sense of dignity. She crawled, she cried, she begged, she pleaded. She tried to grab and hold, but it didn't work. Marsha showed every emotion, every feeling, and stripped herself completely. Her mystique—her pride, her self-esteem—is gone, and so is Henry.

Would their relationship have been any different if Marsha hadn't lost her self-respect and resorted to groveling?

The average man disrespects groveling in a woman. Women disrespect that behavior in a man, too. A woman can't afford to let a man see all of her fears and emotions. She must maintain an aura of mystery. Who knows what the outcome might have been if Marsha hadn't been so transparent?

The man I mentioned earlier, who had been unfaithful to

his wife, said this of his mistress, "I guess her attraction to me is there is always something more to know." Maybe that is the essence of what we're talking about. The woman has qualities that we can't see. Let's take another case in point.

The Mysterious Other Woman

Lana, a recent divorcée and mother of two teenage sons, told me this story:

> I recently met his new wife and felt terribly jealous. I could understand if she was young and sexy, but she isn't. Maria isn't especially beautiful, and she's older than I am. "What does she have that I don't?" I asked him. Then I was sorry I had.
>
> He looked at me and shook his head. "I'm not sure," he began. "You're prettier, in some ways. But you're ... you don't ..." He took a deep breath and tried again. "Lana, you're like a book I've read a hundred times. Nothing ever changes, and I just got tired of reading. Maria intrigues me," he continued. "It's as if I can never come to the end of her. Maria's like an ocean—full of mystery. I get the feeling it would take more than a lifetime to fathom her depths. She makes me feel important; she listens to me. But most of all, Maria has ... happiness, an inner joy that bubbles up from inside her. Nothing seems to keep her down."
>
> When he finished, I wanted to hate him and Maria—an old book, indeed! But I couldn't. The truth is, I like her. If I were a man and had to make a choice between Maria and me, I'd choose Maria. The truth hurts.

We need to understand a specific difference between men and women. Regardless of the tremendous achievements women have made throughout the centuries, most of us enjoy a certain amount of security and sameness. Men, on the other hand, usually strive for adventure. It is as if men were born to conquer, to seek and search, to always face a challenge.

Naturally, there has always been an invisible force that draws men to women and women to men. Young girls are fascinating creatures to boys. They are steeped in mystery. While the boys may know the anatomical facts, they are intrigued by the tremendous power girls have over them and by all the secrets of femininity they don't yet understand—not only sexually, but in their personalities, as well.

With ten to twenty-five years of marriage, much of that mystery has been revealed. And while we want our husbands to know us, I don't think it's wise to completely obliterate that sense of mystery.

If a man knows everything about his wife and she stops developing, what is there left to stimulate him? A woman can't afford to sit back in the comfort and security of her home. She has to grow; she has to learn the secret of mystique, or she just might lose her husband to a woman like Maria.

Perhaps you are asking, "But how is it possible to remain a mystery to your husband? When you live together, sleep together, how can he not know all about you? Besides, I want him to know me intimately."

I've been married to my husband, Lyall, for fifty years. He knows me intimately, yet there is still some mystery in our relationship. Because we are continually learning and growing, neither of us can ever really catch up with the other. I have thoughts and feelings he doesn't know and never will know about.

When I said that to one group of ladies, the question was asked, "How can you keep things from your husband? Isn't that deceptive?"

"Oh, I don't think so," I said. "Actually I think it would be absolutely klutzy of us to reveal everything. There must be some carefully guarded parts of our inner selves. You don't tell your husband every thought that passes through your head, do you? I certainly don't. I always want to have an element of surprise."

Mystique Is . . .

Let's consider Maria for a moment. What does she have that we don't? How can we be more like her?

To some of us, Maria seems too good to be true. Have you ever seen women like her who seem to have it all together? They have the same struggles and trials all the rest of us do, but somehow they seem more resilient, more able to bounce back and handle their problems.

Maria and women like her are what I like to call women of mystique. Unfortunately, women like this send many of us into a deep depression and tend to lower our self-esteem. But let's not compare her positives with our negatives and cry over our failures. Instead, let's have a look at those positive attributes and principles and learn to apply them to our own lives.

I can't think of a better place to begin than by defining *mystique*. According to Webster, *mystique* is "an air or attitude of mystery and reverence developing around something."

When I talk to people about mystique, I'm often asked, "But isn't it manipulative to purposely be aloof or charming to make yourself more appealing to a man?"

My answer is no. I don't believe developing mystique is manipulative. Is it manipulative to learn computer technology? Learning about computers when they aren't a natural part of your personality is a challenge, a means of expanding your interests. When a woman learns mystique, she is developing her charm, her beauty, her self-esteem. She is expanding her interests. A woman of mystique has a quiet inner confidence.

What it all boils down to is motive. A woman must ask

herself, "Am I learning mystique to manipulate others, or am I trying to improve my relationships?"

Who Has Mystique?

I hesitate to use famous people as examples because all we ever see of them is their good side or what gossips say about them. Some of them may be horrid and quite naughty in private. But my examples do have some special qualities that draw people to them, and we can learn from them, even if they're not perfect.

Let me go back to the illustration I used at the beginning of this chapter. Mrs. Wallis Simpson, divorcée and woman of the world, was not considered an acceptable wife for the king, but obviously she was a woman of mystique. What was it about her that made her so special? She was certainly no beauty, although she did have class. It is said that she gave the king something no one else could: her undying faithfulness, and confidence in himself.

Another woman who comes to my mind, also a historical figure, is Jenny Churchill. It is said of her that even at seventy-two, all men were intrigued by her. She was utterly marvelous, charming, gracious, and stylish.

More modern women of mystique might include Estee Lauder, of cosmetic fame, Joanne Wallace, popular Christian speaker and writer, Katharine Hepburn, Jackie Kennedy Onassis, Nancy Reagan, and perhaps Princess Diana (although she's still a bit young).

Not all women of mystique are famous and as we study the attributes of a woman of mystique, perhaps you'll recognize some of your own friends.

More Than a Pretty Face

One of the most prominent attributes seen in women of mystique is beauty. Perhaps *beauty* is not quite the right word here, as our society has misconstrued the word's true meaning. We've come to think of beauty as the pretty young faces that adorn the TV ads or parade through beauty pageants.

Actually, a woman may be beautiful yet not have an especially pretty face. Her beauty is in the elegant way she carries herself, her self-assuredness, her style.

A good example might be Barbra Streisand. She was rejected during her early theater career on the basis of her physical appearance. Instead of being drawn to her talents, shallow show managers saw only her outward appearance—a skinny kid with a big nose. They said she'd never make it, with her profile.

We can laugh now; she's one of the highest paid entertainers around. Her profile's still the same, but who notices? When I think of Barbra, I see a talented, beautiful woman.

Just as beauty does not require a flawless face, neither does it require youth. Most women of mystique are over forty. Being a true woman of mystique requires maturity and wisdom. There is an agelessness about her appearance and attitude; she lives as though life has no end.

Your Gotta Have Style

Part of a woman's beauty is her style. I'm not talking about fashion. A woman of mystique is never trendy, but she develops her own individual style. She compensates for what she doesn't have by accentuating her positives.

Today we have no excuse for not developing our own style. We can wear anything we want and are no longer tied to trendy fashion.

There are wonderful books and seminars available for women, where we can learn about the colors, styles, and makeup that best suit us. For example, books like Joanne Wallace's *Dress With Style* and *Image of Loveliness*, or Marita

Littauer's book, *Shades of Beauty*, can be a great help. I have
seen thousands of women turn from frumpy to fabulous
after a little effort on their part.

Contrary to popular belief, a woman doesn't need a lot of
clothes to have style. In fact, the famous Lillie Langtry made
her debut in London in the 1890's with only one simple but
elegant black dress, which had been designed by a French
dressmaker from her village. Lillie, with that one basic
dress, aroused the admiration of the greatest painters of her
day. While other women of her day had elaborate ward-
robes, she startled her audiences and entranced a king by
her elegance in black.

Don't let the lack of money keep you from developing an
attractive outward appearance. You may not be out to im-
press kings and princes with your great beauty, but
wouldn't it be nice to feel and look stunning? Start with one
dress or outfit in which you look absolutely marvelous and
build from there.

Perhaps you're thinking, *I have terrible taste in clothes*. If,
like Charlie the Tuna, your taste leaves something to be de-
sired, ask a well-dressed friend to help you.

Improving your appearance improves your self-esteem. I
am living proof of that. When I first started speaking, I
didn't bother about my appearance. I simply wanted to be
appreciated for my "wisdom." I wore anything, including
cheap polyester pantsuits. Today, after much coaching from
my friends, I am learning how to dress in a more attractive
manner.

I feel ever so much better about myself. It's a thrill to
have someone stop me, as one woman did the other day.
"You look great! Pink really is your color. I hope I look as
good as you when I'm your age."

I've had women ask me why I put so much emphasis on
appearance. "After all," they say, "it's what's inside that
counts."

Yes, that's true. But remember, like it or not, men are stimulated by attractive women. They are generally very visual, and don't like sloppy women. A man wants to be proud of his wife or date. Most normal men like their women to be admired, because it literally enhances their own ego.

Now be honest: Don't you like your husband to look good? A woman wants to be proud of her man, too. Personally, I think it's a sick man—one who is prone to jealousy and possessiveness—who doesn't want his wife or date to be admired. The healthy man loves to have his wife admired and envied by others.

If not for a man, be beautiful for yourself. Looking good usually leads to feeling good.

Mystique and a Healthy Glow

Speaking of feeling good: A woman of mystique will have a glow about her, an inner beauty that comes from taking care of her body.

Perhaps when you think of women of mystique in terms of health, certain women come to mind. I think of Stormie Omartian, who is a popular singer known nationwide for her aerobics done to Christian music.

Other names that come to mind are Jane Fonda and Linda Evans. These women have stamina, an inner glow, determination, and discipline—traits that set them apart from other women.

As an avid reader of historical biographies, I have studied many famous women of the past. One woman in particular comes to mind. Diane de Poitiers was an adored friend of Prince Henry of France, who became Henry II of France. She was twenty years older than he, yet he loved her and was faithful to her until the day he died. She remained lovely into her old age, and it is said her unwaning beauty was related to the way she cared for her body.

She exercised and took cold baths every day and dieted on the finest and freshest of foods money could buy. She was a brilliant woman in her time.

Feeling good inside and out can do wonders in lifting your spirits, even when your hormones are threatening to send you into another storm.

Beauty Creates Energy

"What do you do to lift yourself up out of the blues?" I asked a group of ladies in a support group I attended. We'd gathered that day to talk about overcoming depression.

"Oh, I go shopping," said Emily. "I try on all the lovely clothes I can't afford—minks, sequined dresses. Then I treat myself to lunch at Alexander's. The antiques and beautiful table settings and French waiters make me feel . . . elegant. I suppose it sounds silly, but I always go home feeling better."

"No," I said, "I don't think it's silly at all. You are surrounding yourself with beauty, and that makes you feel good. When I'm in a sore mood, I go out and pick or buy flowers. Then, as I arrange them and set them in their place, I admire them. I can almost feel the frustration or anger or depression flow out of me."

"I know what you mean," said Laura, one of the younger women. "I feel the same way when I go for a walk in the woods. I let my mind drift to all the beautiful things God made, and pretty soon I'm feeling at peace again."

Without even realizing it, these women recognized the human need for beauty. In my studies I realized a fascinating truth: Women of mystique create beauty around them. They somehow recognize the tremendous human need for loveliness.

This basic need is often overlooked in our busy lives. We know our basic needs include food, clothing, shelter, and perhaps companionship, but seldom consider beauty a necessary item.

I think God knows how important beauty is to us. We have but to open our eyes to know He wanted us to be surrounded by beautiful things.

During the war we lived in Australia. One of the block wardens, a friend of ours, told us an interesting story. He was concerned because people were resisting his instructional meetings on air raids, blackouts, and first aid. He said he'd finally chosen a day when he felt nearly everyone in the neighborhood would be free. When he announced the meeting day, do you know what the women said? "Oh, no! That's the day I buy my flowers. That's my flower arranging day."

With Japanese submarines in the bay and danger all around them, these women wouldn't give up their flower arranging. I'm sure they didn't consciously realize it, but in the midst of trouble, those flowers were basic to their well-being.

Think about how you feel when beauty surrounds you, and when it doesn't. Imagine yourself sitting on the steps of a tenement house. You yawn with lazy despair. The ground is nearly bare, with an occasional clump of weeds cut to resemble grass. Garbage oozes over an open garbage can. You bend to pull one of the millions of weeds growing in the cracks of the walk that leads into the litter-lined street. Graffiti covers the fence; the words written in iridescent green make you turn away.

The housing development is only four years old and already the paint is chipped and peeling on the once white windowsills. Black soot covers the orange-red bricks. Your attention is brought back to the street as a passing truck driver hurls obscenities at a small child who crouches in the gutter to gather more stones. You wish you could wipe it all away, but it's too much . . . too hard.

Not a pretty sight. Lack of beauty—ugliness—brings grief to the spirit. Shabbiness and disorder drain us.

Now imagine the same place. A woman moves in next door. She scrubs and cleans inside and out, then sands and paints the trim a sparkling white. She waters the parched and patchy yard and scatters grass seed. Maybe by now you feel a bit guilty and intrigued by the small but effective changes she's made. You ask if she'd mind if you worked together. She laughs and hands you a rake. Together you plant flowers and shrubs. You gather discarded bricks and create a garden full of forget-me-nots and candytufts. The child stops throwing rocks and comes to watch. You hand him a packet of seeds, and he smiles.

Can you feel the difference? Beauty creates energy. It lifts the spirit.

I did a survey a few years ago with 150 couples. I asked the men to list, in order, those things about their wives and home life that upset them the most. More men complained about bad housekeeping than about cooking, sex, or their wives' appearance. Men also have a need for a beautiful and tidy environment.

Contrary to what you may be thinking, it doesn't take a lot of money to create beauty. I have never been a woman of affluence. For some years during the Depression, we were quite poor. Yet my children recently told me they'd never realized it. I always set the dining room table with a linen cloth and china and nearly always arranged a centerpiece of fresh flowers on the table. Perhaps because of my British upbringing, I stressed proper table manners. Even though we had little money, I tried to give my family a lovely environment whenever possible.

Beauty Debriefs Tension

As I said earlier, beauty calms the spirit. Tension, anxiety, stress, depression, anger—all can be defused by beauty. As a counselor, I have a tendency to internalize my patients' problems. I may come out of a session tight with tension. Often I will take some time and go to a quiet place and glory in loveliness. Other times, when I can't go out, I close my eyes and let my imagination create a beautiful scene. One I use often is the picture I see when I recite Wordsworth's poem "The Daffodils." I've never really seen the exact place he talks about, but my imagination brings it to life, and I find rest in the beauty of his words.

> For oft, when on my couch I lie
> In vacant or in pensive mood,
> They flash upon that inward eye
> Which is the bliss of solitude;
> And then my heart with pleasure fills,
> And dances with the daffodils.

A woman of mystique is one who "dances with the daffodils" and brings others into the dance with her.

The Trouble With Honesty

There is one attribute of the woman of mystique that I almost hesitate to bring up, and that is honesty. I could get into trouble here, but I'm old enough that I don't have to worry about it. Honesty is not always the best policy.

How can I say that? Because I have seen too many relationships destroyed in the name of honesty. Complete honesty in any relationship can at times be destructive and brutal.

While I'll be the first to say we shouldn't be dishonest or deceitful, there are some things more important than blurting out the truth or our honest opinions. To clarify, let me give you an example.

At the end of the sixties we were plunged into the world

of encounter groups. Many businesses felt it suddenly important that their staff members participate in encounter groups, which were designed to relieve tension and help us get along better with fellow workers by expressing our feelings in total honesty.

We had these encounter sessions where I worked and were led by a so-called expert to confront one another. In turn, we would each tell what we liked and disliked about each person in the group. It was devastating. Many of the more diligent participants were young people, who thought they were being forthright and helpful with their honest and sometimes brutal attacks.

If you were mature, you supposedly could handle the criticisms hurled against you by "loving people who cared." As far as I am concerned, all the maturity and wisdom in the world weren't enough to keep those sharp words from piercing the heart.

I wouldn't have dared express what I felt toward some of those young people. Knowing how I and some of my colleagues felt, I knew the truth would hurt them far more than they realized. There were brash, impulsive, insensitive, and insulting words released in the name of honesty.

In many firms these groups caused havoc. People withdrew because they couldn't take the chance of being visible and therefore vulnerable to criticism. Trust among employees diminished.

This experience is one of the reasons I often advise against confrontation. Of course, encounter groups can be valuable, and they have their place. But extreme care must be taken to be sensitive to other people. I would be the last to deny honesty, but timing, tact, mercy, and compassion must take first priority.

For instance, say I feel very angry with someone who has wronged me. I want to rush in and confront him. But before

I do, I must stop and say, "What will my confrontation do to that person?" And also, "What will it do to our relationship?"

Several years ago Margaret came to me for counseling. "I said some terrible things to my husband. I told him I hated his stupid jokes and stupid crooked smile. I was so angry I told him I never wanted to see him again. Oh, Jean . . . he walked out and said I didn't have to worry, he wouldn't be back."

She sniffed loudly, and I handed her another tissue. "Go on," I said.

"Well, after he left I just sat there. It's been two weeks, and he hasn't even called. I didn't mean what I said. He does have a crooked smile, but it's adorable and . . . I miss him."

As it turned out, Margaret had been premenstrual during her attack. Not that PMS excused her behavior, but it did explain a few things. Her husband finally contacted her and agreed to have a try at saving the marriage.

Margaret's behavior was rather brash and utterly "umystiquey." Her honest confrontation nearly destroyed her marriage.

Many times during a particularly emotional or stressful time of the monthly cycle or life cycle, you may have negative feelings about your spouse, another family member, or friend. Being completely honest at these times can, as Margaret discovered, destroy a marriage or relationship.

I know it's hard to avoid clashes where words slip out and are later regretted. We must remember that the tongue can be a weapon more biting than a bullet. Once words are shot off the tongue, they can never be taken back.

The tongue can get us into all sorts of trouble. It can gossip, criticize, nag, whine, and complain—all of which are quite unbecoming. A true woman of mystique will learn to guard her tongue and use it wisely.

The Way of a Woman With a Man

I'd like to go a bit further with this thought on guarding the tongue. Over the years, I learned some interesting things about men. One was the things men hate most in women: envy, jealousy, vicious gossip, sloppiness in all forms (though any old body shape was okay), bad moods, depression, or excessive small talk.

One man told me about a woman in his office he had admired. "I asked her to lunch one day," he said. "In an hour, she had bad-mouthed eight people. For some reason I started keeping track. It was awful." Her gossip changed his whole attitude toward her. A woman of mystique doesn't have the luxury of gossiping about people. It's no good looking gorgeous when there are ugly things coming out of your mouth.

A woman of mystique is trusted by others. She shows herself to be a good friend and confidante. She works at being interesting, intelligent, and charming.

By the way, let me tell you a story that comes to mind about a girls' school I went to that taught charm as part of the curriculum. All the girls in my class were "coming out" (a British custom for introducing young debutantes to society).

Because they were having great weekends of social gatherings, parties, and dates, all during the week the girls worked on their "stocks," which were topics of conversation that a girl might fall back on when talking with the opposite sex.

We'd study the latest cricket scores, the newest model cars, international affairs, at least one good classic piece of literature. Monday morning the girls used to race into class early and say, "Did you have to fall back on many?"

You didn't always need your stocks to charm a man, but

it was good to have all those topics you'd studied on hand when the conversation got dull.

The young ladies in my day knew a lot more about working to charm a man. I'm sure young people of today would sneer at that as being a bit manipulative, but I don't think so. I think it's good, solid preparation for knowing how to keep a man interested for a lifetime.

I'd like to add one more quality here having to do with charm, and that is letting a man save face. A woman of mystique knows better than to win all the arguments, especially those argued in public. Have you ever been at a social event where a woman is winning a point with a man and watched his embarrassment? It's an uncomfortable situation. I'm not saying a woman should be a doormat and never push her point. I'm simply suggesting that as a general rule it is unwise to belittle a man, even if it means losing or giving up the argument.

I know it's a controversial subject, especially with so many women learning assertiveness and moving into top-level executive positions, but like it or not, most men will run away from a woman who is, in his mind, overly aggressive. He doesn't see her as being clever. We're not talking about what's fair and reasonable here; we're talking about the natural way of a man.

Aggression is warlike and has most generally been thought of as a male trait. And while I certainly think women need to be strong and assertive (which means a gentle standing up for your rights and beliefs), we must also be careful we don't push too far or at the wrong time.

That doesn't mean we need to stop climbing to top-level business positions. On the contrary, it simply means that we relax, use our brains, and let our feminine mystique go to work for us. Men don't usually like women who develop masculine traits in order to succeed in business, but they do respect women who are women.

Dipping Into the Pool of Knowledge

The women of mystique whom I have studied and have known seem to have an unquenchable thirst for knowledge. They never cease to learn, never cease to add to their growing wisdom.

A woman who dips deep and often into the pool of knowledge can never be as Lana's exhusband described her—an old book. Rather she will be like a library filled with intriguing books that one can't put down. Her desire to experience life and partake continually of the pool of knowledge separates her from boredom and self-pity. It creates in her a wellspring that others come to for refreshment.

Every morning brings a new, fresh, empty page in your book. What will you have written on it at the end of the day? What new things will you have learned?

Dr. James Dobson recently asked me, "But don't many women go off to work for that reason? Isn't that encouraging women to put the family in a lower priority?"

"Heavens, no," I said. "Women who choose to stay home in a homemaking career and keep their family in high priority still have a tremendous opportunity to learn."

When I lived in Australia, Lyall and I had three small children. It was during the war, and we had none of the modern conveniences. We didn't even have hot water—I had to heat it in a large copper kettle. Yet, by organizing my time, I managed to spend two hours a day in a disciplined study program.

A woman of mystique never stops learning, for to do so means stagnation, and how long can a man drink from a stagnant pool?

Wit and Winsomeness

There is something contagious about a smile. I'm sure most of you have seen the *Mona Lisa* and heard the song about her famous smile. How intriguing and inviting is that smile.

There is something captivating in a woman who possesses a sense of humor. One of the things we must never lose as we continue through the phases of our lives is laughter. No matter how severe the storm, no matter how fiery your ordeal, for sanity's sake, don't let go of laughter.

Sometimes I get so tied up, so tense, I feel like screaming. You know, like you'd wind up a toy and hold it at its breaking point. Then someone, usually one of the children, will say or do something funny, and I laugh. The laughter feels like someone's let the windup mechanism go. The tension fades. Laughter heals.

A woman of mystique seldom zeros in on her own needs, but works to lift depression in others. She provides good cheer, and others often find her amusing. Men especially enjoy this quality, as they don't like being dumped on. They have a hard time coping with women's needs and moods. Yes, they *should* learn to understand a woman's needs and moods and help her through some of her struggles, but they don't especially like it. A woman of mystique is careful to develop a balance and not overwhelm her man with troubles and burdens. She uses her wit and winsomeness to lighten heavy situations. She can laugh at herself and her mistakes.

Spirituality: the Essence of Mystique

This final attribute is perhaps the most important. It is what puts the joy in Maria's heart and makes her deep as an ocean. It is the base on which all the other attributes can be built. Without it, our striving for higher self-esteem, happiness, health, and victory over our problems would be in vain.

A woman of mystique has an inner calm and confidence.

She loves herself and her body and portrays the essence of God, in whose image she was created. This is perhaps the aura of mystery that is missing in so many women. A true woman of mystique has within her being a spiritual realm, filled with a loving God who gives her strength to cope with any situation.

She is constantly changing and growing. She is a mystery to men and women because she involves herself deeply in the things of God.

Her days are spent in learning God's ways and carrying out His will for her life through Bible study and prayer. She is in love with life, celebrating each moment, each day, as if it were her last. She is vital, growing, alive, and filled with the Spirit of God. She is a mystery because God is mystery and His Spirit lives in her.

Our woman of mystique is by no means perfect. She is fully aware of her flaws and weaknesses, yet she is strong enough to admit them and not be embarrassed by them.

She may be vulnerable, yet she possesses the strength to overcome all things. She may have problems, but she possesses the spirit to rise above them. She will rise on the crest of the wave, rather than be thrust to the ground and crushed by the sea's troubled water.

Perhaps a good illustration of a woman of mystique would be the virtuous woman in Proverbs 31. The woman acclaimed as a great wife and mother worked hard and was skilled in many areas. She managed her home and finances well. Her husband was proud of her and her children called her blessed.

I know it sounds like I've painted a picture of a woman who is impossible for us mere mortals to live up to. I share all this information on mystique not to make you feel over-whelmed or guilty, but to help you grow. I know it looks unattainable, especially when you see all these virtuous attributes in one place. But I'd encourage you to go back to the beginning. Work on one thing at a time. Ask God to help you grow in the way He has chosen for you.

All of the attitudes and attributes we talked of earlier work together to build confidence and self-esteem. They can provide strength to help pull us through the emotional and physical ups and downs of our ever-changing phases.

Possessing the qualities of the woman of mystique isn't going to magically transform your life. There are no assurances that even with mystique you'll have a devoted husband and happy-ever-after life. Nothing can guarantee that. But mystique can make you feel better about yourself, make you a more appealing, more interesting, more exciting person to yourself and to others around you.

Part IV

The Menopause ———— ᠔

The menopause phase of our lives can be likened to autumn. It is a time when the reproductive system, like autumn leaves, will wither and die. It is a time of sadness, yet a time of joy. Our childbearing years are nearly over, but there is so much life ahead, so much to look forward to. Menopause is the final transition between youth and maturity. Many of us who have suffered from years of emotional upheaval due to hormonal problems can say, "Soon, very soon, it will be over."

In the next two chapters I'll talk about menopause: its symptoms, its complications, and suggestions to help you ease through your change of life.

14

The Season of Change   ॐ

Jeanette, a 52-year-old woman, called me a short time ago. "Jean, I'm either going through menopause or I've gone crazy."

"So far," I said, "you're sounding normal. What sort of symptoms are you having?"

"Well, I do have some medical problems—high blood pressure, high cholesterol, and now the doctor thinks I have hyperthyroidism. It seems like everything is *up* but me. It isn't the big things that get to me, though. It's the little ones."

"Like what?"

"Well, for one thing, noise of any kind irritates me. I've turned into a nag, always telling my teenage children to turn their radios down or stop squabbling or even stop joking around. I have these strange mood swings. I'll be working along and . . . bingo . . . I'll start crying for no reason at all. There are times when I get this horrid feeling that my husband is seeing another woman. I know it isn't true, and he reassures me that he loves me as much as ever. Another thing: I noticed my voice has swung from soprano to alto. My energy level is sporadic—sometimes I feel so tired. Of course, if I could sleep at night, that might help. I wake up sometimes just drenched and have to change the whole bed. Could that be from hot flashes?

"Jean," she said, "I think I might be going through menopause. My doctor says I'm just overworked and told me I should quit my job. Actually I think he's wrong; it's my work that keeps me from going really crazy."

"I couldn't agree more. Keeping busy can be a great help," I said.

"I thought so, too. But the thought of going through menopause scares me, because my mother had a complete nervous breakdown during her change and was in a mental hospital for months. I'm so afraid that will happen to me."

"First of all," I tried to reassure her, "mothers and daughters don't necessarily follow the same pattern."

"But I'm having the same ups and downs. I feel like a total failure. My self-confidence has dropped completely. I used to be a happy, outgoing person."

"And you probably will be that happy, outgoing person again," I said. "But it might be a good idea for you to consult with another doctor. It never hurts to get a second opinion."

While some women like Jeanette will have a long list of symptoms during menopause, it's also entirely possible you'll feel nothing at all.

Some women wake up one day, realize they have missed several periods in a row, and never have another. About 10 percent of all women claim to have virtually no premenopausal discomfort.

My mother was like that. She and Father went on an ocean voyage. When they returned she missed a period and thought she was pregnant. But there was no pregnancy; she had just gone through her change and never had another menstrual cycle. It shouldn't surprise me, really. My mother, being the proper British woman she was, did everything well.

Since Mother had such an easy time of it, I naturally thought I'd breeze through menopause as well. Not so. Although I had no bothersome physical symptoms, my judgment became very poor. I became obsessed over the welfare of my adult children. I talked incessantly about myself and had a strange, negative kind of depression that never seemed to let up.

If you're among those who are fortunate enough to experience a mild menopause, you may not need the information I'm giving here. However, I would encourage you to read through the material anyway, so you can lend support, encouragement, and help to women who do have a more difficult time.

It's Normal

Before I get into the symptoms of menopause, I'd like to offer three points of encouragement. First of all, we must understand that menopause is a very real and very normal part of our lives. You've known all your life it would happen, and there is nothing you can do to stop it. Yet with the knowledge that you are coming close to menopause comes the knowledge that you are growing older, and perhaps that idea frightens or depresses you.

Contrary to some popular myths of the past, menopause does not signal the end of life. It only means we've reached the end of our childbearing years, and that, my friends, means we enter into a whole new and exciting world. There is life—for me there has been a more abundant life—after menopause.

Second, as one local doctor pointed out, there is a great

deal of literature out now on menopause, and most women are well informed about what to expect. Unfortunately, many women approach their menopausal phase with anxious anticipation. The literature tends to point out all the miserable symptoms that they are likely to have. All this negative input creates a mind-set that causes many women to expect that all these terrible things will happen to them.

Contrary to popular belief, women do not typically go "crazy" during their change of life. In fact, according to an article titled "Hormone Balance in Mid-life" by Dr. Lawrence Galton, a study done on 1,000 women revealed that 50.8 percent reported no acute discomfort with menopausal symptoms. Of those who experienced difficulties, 89.7 percent continued their life and work as usual, with no interruptions. "Only 10.3 percent were truly incapacitated at intervals."[1]

Going through menopause may be every bit as traumatic as going through adolescence, both physically and emotionally. But just as many girls glide easily through puberty, many women have little or no difficulty adjusting to menopause. If symptoms do occur and become difficult to deal with, treatment is available through competent family practitioners and gynecologists.

So often symptoms of premenopause are mingled with other factors. As we learned in the last section, mid-life carries with it a lot of stress. It is important to sort out those problems that may be related to other sources, such as marital difficulties, loneliness, parenting dilemmas, unrelated medical problems, and even PMS.

In order to recognize what is premenopausal and what is not, you'll want a clear understanding of the menopausal phase.

Coming to Terms

You'll remember that we talked about the mid-life mal-aise and how some of the symptoms might possibly be linked to the climacteric, or perimenopause. In the late thirties, it is entirely possible that the ovaries reduced their production of estrogen and for a time everything went haywire. Since the body has a wonderful way of adjusting to change, the adrenal glands may have stepped up their output and temporarily helped rebalance the hormones and your emotions.

As the reproductive system begins to close down, the ovaries put out less and less estrogen, until eventually the physical signs of estrogen deficiency appear. Perimenopause, or climacteric, is a gradual process. Normally, the process begins around the age of thirty-eight and ends around fifty-five. There are exceptions, of course:

Premature menopause   Menopause (complete cessation of the menstrual cycle) occurring before the age of forty.

Surgical menopause   Menopause beginning immediately following the surgical removal of both ovaries. Women who have one remaining ovary can expect to go through a normal menopause.

Late menopause   Menopause after sixty. Apparently, since we have a longer life expectancy than many cultures, late menopause is not uncommon among American women. Yet women who experience menstrual flow after sixty years of age are at a high risk for endometrial cancer. Most doctors recommend these women undergo an endometrial biopsy or D & C every year or two.[2]

During perimenopause, the decline in estrogen production is usually gradual, taking about four or five years. The adrenal glands, however, continue to produce estrogen, but at lower levels. Additional estrogen is supplied by another hormone, androstenedione. This is a weak male hormone produced by the ovaries and adrenals. A woman's body fat converts part of this hormone into estrogen, but even with this addition, estrogen will probably be in short supply, and the body may require estrogen replacement therapy.

Eventually the body adjusts to this lower level of estrogen. Before the adjustment, the control center of the brain, the hypothalamus, can get a bit confused, causing some unpleasant symptoms.

Some Menopausal Facts

In our country today we have over 40 million women who have safely made the transition from premenopause to postmenopause. You might be interested in some statistics I've gathered on menopause.

The average age of cessation of menstrual function is 52 years. About 30 percent of women will have had menopause by the time they are 45, and 98 percent will have had menopause by the time they are 55.[3]

It is estimated that 75 to 80 percent of women will develop symptoms due to estrogen withdrawal.

Premenopause can begin as early as 35 or be delayed until the age of 60. The average range is between 45 and 55. Women whose menses stop before 45 years of age are said to have a premature menopause.

Individuals vary greatly in when premenopause begins and the length of time it takes for the transition to be complete. But there are some factors that may indicate whether you will have an early or late menopause.

Some sources say there is no connection between when a woman starts her menses and when menses end. But Katharina Dalton, in her book *Once a Month*, says there is. She says those who start menstruation early tend to finish late, and those who begin late tend to finish early.[4]

Women who have had a lifetime of low estrogen output, Dr. Dalton says, "have a tendency to finish menstruation before the average. On the other hand PMS sufferers usually finish after 50 years of age."[5]

There may be some genetic factors involved, too. A family of women—mother, daughter, sister, aunt—may all end their menstrual cycles early or late. This is unusual, however, and I've found you can't really count on similarity among family members.

According to Dr. Dalton, a survey of forty-eight- to forty-nine-year-old postmenopausal women found that a high percentage were smokers. This suggests that smoking could lead to earlier menopause.[6]

Basically, the effect of estrogen loss depends largely on your own genetic resistance to aging, your overall health, quality of diet, and activity.

Physical Symptoms of Menopause

Now it's time to have a look at some of the somatic (physical) symptoms associated with menopause.

Erratic menstrual cycles A woman might experience a very gradual ending, where periods are regular but last for fewer days. Another woman may complain of erratic periods, missing one occasionally and then gradually missing more and more. For some women, like my mother, there may be a sudden cessation of menstruation.

Hot flashes or flushes These are burning sensations usually beginning from the waist and moving to the top of the head. Outwardly the skin might be flushed and beads of sweat may appear. Along with the flush, a woman might have a fluttering in the chest or palpitations, apprehension, or anxiety attacks. A flush will last only a few minutes. They may range from one to two a week up to one hundred a day. This is one of the most common complaints of premenopausal women and is often the source of much embarrassment.

Hot flashes frequently occur at night. The flush is uncomfortable, and the woman awakens to find herself completely drenched. This phenomenon is referred to as night sweats.

Insomnia and consequent tiredness This is a common complaint as well, and may be due to sleepless nights resulting from hot flashes or other premenopausal problems, as well as emotional upsets.

Vaginal dryness Dryness and atrophy of the genital tissue may be due to a lack of estrogen. This may lead to vaginitis, itching, irritation of the vaginal area, pain, urinary frequency, and pain during intercourse. These symptoms may cause a decreased interest in sex.

Bladder changes The bladder and bladder opening become thinner. The bladder may not empty properly. This condition can lead to cystitis (urinary tract infections) and leaking. The muscle that holds urine in often becomes weak, and a simple cough or sneeze releases an unexpected flood of urine.

Loss of fatty tissue and decreased muscle tone May lead to a collapse of vaginal walls. Occasionally women end up with a prolapsed uterus, which may require reparative surgery.

Dry skin The skin often becomes dry, pale, and thin, losing its elasticity and contributing to wrinkling, especially around the eyes, mouth, and neck.

Breast changes Breasts may sag from a decrease in fat cells and muscle tone.

Unusual skin sensations One rather odd symptom that's been reported by premenopausal women is a creepy-crawly sensation on the skin. In a letter I received recently, a pastor's wife shared a story about a friend whose cat is being treated for a hormone deficiency because she was spayed too young. "The cat kept pulling her fur out with her teeth, thinking that things were crawling on her skin," she writes. "The cat has to take hormones! Maybe I ought to go to a veterinarian for my scalp condition!" Sad to think that felines at times get more attention and better treatment than women.

Other symptoms Often related to estrogen deficiency are dizziness, weight gain, bloating, and gastrointestinal disturbances such as constipation and diarrhea.

Calcium deficiency Loss or fluctuation of calcium levels may bring on osteoporosis, and arthriticlike pains may develop in the bones. Women in premenopause often complain of joint stiffness and leg cramps. These pains may be due to a lack of calcium.

More on Osteoporosis

Estrogen deficiency has been linked to a progressive and serious bone disease called osteoporosis. Lately there has been much literature written on osteoporosis. Today it is a widely accepted theory that much of the bone deterioration seen in postmenopausal women in their seventies is due to a lack of estrogen.

Researchers now feel that problems such as shortened, deformed, and misaligned spines; the "dowager's hump," or bow at the top of the spine; and fragile bones that lead to frequent fractures can often be lessened with estrogen replacement therapy.

Symptoms Vary

Again, not everyone goes through premenopause in the same way. Dr. Penny Wise Budoff, in her book *No More Menstrual Cramps and Other Good News* says:

> There is a marked individual variation in the amount and proportion of the remaining hormones the ovaries produce, as well as in the total length of time that this occurs. This is why some women have severe symptoms, while others have few complaints.
>
> Women with more fat tend to be able to convert more androstenedione to estrogen and have fewer symptoms. Some women may never become symptomatic: they may produce hormones over a longer period of time and have a slower waning of the entire process.[7]

I'll be going into some treatments and helps for surviving the premenopause in the next chapter. But first let's take a look at the emotional upheaval often accompanying the fluctuating hormone levels in premenopausal women.

Growing Older: Growing Better

Unfortunately, premenopause directly coincides with or follows mid-life malaise. Let's face it: Menopause couldn't happen at a more inconvenient time. Unfortunately, in

many women the feelings about menopause are not happy
ones. Perhaps they haven't yet been able to let go of the
dream of youth. Perhaps they haven't yet come to the other
side of mid-life. Whatever the cause, they come into premenopause uncertain, unsure of their roles, and frightened
about the future.

Paula, a woman of 55, married for twenty-five years with
four children, decided one day to run away from home with
a man fifteen years younger than herself. "She had been
growing increasingly restless," her husband told me. "I
should have seen trouble coming when she started dressing
differently. She wore more makeup, dressed more like a girl
in her teens than a woman. Then one day she just announced she was leaving. She said I was too old for her, that
this guy made her feel young again."

Paula was trying to fight for her youth. One day she'll
wake up to find that age has won the battle after all. I've
never been able to understand this obsession to hold onto
youth.

Actually, society has recently been entertaining the no-
tion that older people can be beautiful. There has been a lot
of attention given to glamorous women over forty—women
like Linda Evans, Jane Fonda, Joan Collins, and *The Golden
Girls* of the weekly television program. In a way, this is
great. We see role models and positive affirmations of older
people achieving and maintaining success.

The new vision of what a woman over forty can be creates a few problems, though. These older television women
flaunt their good looks, sex appeal, and the fact that they are
over forty and still gorgeous. These women, as portrayed
for all the world to see, are rich and beautiful, adored by
men of all ages, have no hot flashes, depression, snappy
moods, or crying spells, and appear wonderfully in control
of their lives and their men.

Nevertheless, as on TV, there are many women who have

successfully transitioned through their mid-life malaise. They are revived, reborn, and ready to move on with fresh goals. They actually look forward to growing older and seem perfectly happy as they watch their hair gray and their wrinkles deepen. There is a sparkle in their eyes as their children's offspring call them Grandma.

But for each woman who ages happily and gracefully, there are half a dozen who mourn every birthday past forty. They bring out the black balloons, black T-shirts, black coffee cups, all covered with sayings like "I'm over the hill."

I hate that saying. For one thing, I don't believe a word of it. Life doesn't stop at forty—it *starts*. That's when climbing the mountain of life really gets interesting!

The Emotional Side of Menopause

Emotional stresses arise when women don't understand the association between their strange emotional upsets and their hormonal imbalance. Although emotions can and often are separate from our hormones, they can also be very much connected.

Emotions fluctuate, as do the changing hormone levels. They vary from woman to woman, depending on mental and physical health, attitudes, background, and relationships. I've listed some of the most common symptoms below.

• Feeling less feminine. Part of this feeling is due to the woman's knowledge that she is becoming sterile and can no longer have a baby. It may also be due to the fact that with the decline in female hormones, male hormones can become more prominent, causing the growth of dark, coarse facial hair.

• Fear of growing older and losing her attractiveness and sexuality.

• Irritability. Many women complain about being easily upset and having low tolerance of noise, activity, and small children.

• Anxiety and tension headaches are a frequent complaint among premenopausal women.

• Hyperactivity, the feeling of constantly having to be on the move, is experienced by some.

• Low self-esteem is probably one of the most common problems in women approaching menopause. They worry about their physical appearance, but also their sexuality and their mental and emotional stability. They may spend much time in introspection about their past failures, which seem to qualify the way they feel about themselves now.

• Depression is high on the list of symptoms and can vary from a bout with the blues to a full-scale depression complete with thoughts of suicide.

• Some women say they react at times with inappropriate emotional responses. Many experience sudden and unaccountable mood changes.

• A premenopausal woman often needs proof of love. She may become suspicious, and paranoid, of her husband and friends and feel people are plotting against her.

• Interference with sleep is an all too common complaint, generally due to hot flashes and night sweats.

• Some women say they have difficulty with concentration and experience forgetfulness.

• There may be a feeling of loneliness arising from the fact that the woman may be facing an empty nest, with her children grown and gone.

• Women often express a loss of libido or sexual desire. This may in part be due to the thinning out and dryness of the vaginal tissue.

These symptoms might seem overwhelming, but bear in mind that not everyone has all of them, and some women have very few. Even those who suffer the full course of symptoms generally survive. Menopause, after all, is not fatal; but it certainly can be frustrating.

Often women suffer needlessly, when with understanding, proper treatment, and a physician's care, they could lead a normal life. It is important for us to go into menopause with a feeling of self-worth, knowing our lives are not ending as we pass through this transition, but that a new and exciting phase is beginning.

The emotional and hormonal instability during menopause is the bad news. The good news is: Eventually, it will end. And the even better news is that with estrogen therapy, the premenopausal and postmenopausal years don't have to play havoc with our lives.

Menopause is nothing to be afraid of. I sort of looked forward to it, and I hope you will, too. It's simply one of those rocks in life that we must either climb over or find a way around. Since there is no way around menopause, I suggest you take a deep breath and commence climbing.

15

Managing Menopause ᜒ

Years ago, women suffering with premenopausal symptoms were simply ignored unless their symptoms became serious enough for them to be sent to a psychiatrist, where they would often be given tranquilizers or at times even shock therapy.

Today, at least among the more up-to-date family practitioners and gynecologists, menopause is considered a "disease process" that must be followed up by medical care in order to prevent a series of life-threatening maladies such as osteoporosis. I thoroughly dislike using the word *disease* in connection with menopause. I'd rather think of it as a developmental phase. But I suppose we shouldn't worry too much about what the medical profession calls it, as long as they do something about it.

Most doctors see medical intervention as a must, unless their patient is producing adequate amounts of estrogen on her own. In this chapter we'll examine the various treatments and helps for women in the premenopausal phase of their lives.

See Your Doctor

If you suspect you are entering menopause—especially if you are having a difficult time with some of the symptoms we discussed—I'd recommend an examination.

Learn all you can about menopause and the appropriate and generally accepted forms of treatment before you go. Then feel free to discuss your symptoms. Find out what your doctor's approach is to menopause. How does he feel about it? What is his attitude? How does he treat his menopausal patients?

In order to evaluate your doctor, ask him to explain menopause to you. You'll be able to tell if he really cares for you and will work with you or if he considers premenopausal women a pain in his cervical vertebrae.

If you feel uncomfortable with the doctor, if he doesn't give you adequate explanations, if he doesn't believe in estrogen therapy, or if he takes you and your problems too lightly, get a second opinion.

Diet, Exercise, and Other Necessary Helps

If you have not already reviewed your eating habits and exercise program, I suggest you do so now. The dietary suggestions I've given in previous chapters still apply, perhaps even more so now. Naturally, the way we take care of our bodies in the first half of our lives will directly affect how our bodies treat us during the second half. Unfortunately, we have to live with the logical consequences of our actions.

It's not too late, however. Shaping up your body and your eating habits can make your mature years happier, healthier, and more fun.

There are a couple of points I'd like to make about dietary needs in the last phases of our lives. The first may be helpful in preventing osteoporosis.

According to Dr. McIlhaney, "Before menopause, women need to have about 1,000 mg. of calcium a day; after menopause they need 1,500 mg. daily." Since the normal calcium consumption in a balanced diet is 400–500 mg. a day, women should supplement with one or two 250 mg. calcium pills with breakfast and one or two with the evening meal. Dr. McIlhaney cautions that some calcium preparations contain vitamin D. Since we usually get plenty of vitamin D with sunshine, we don't need more. "The intake of more than 1,000 units of vitamin D a day," he says, "may actually cause bone loss. . . ." Also, more than 5,000 units of vitamin A a day is known to cause bone loss.

Of the calciums available, Os-Cal, Caltrate 600, BioCal, and also Tums antacid, are good sources of calcium carbonate. Dr. McIlhaney cautions women to avoid two sources of calcium—bone meal and dolomite, since they both contain lead.[1]

The following is a rather controversial subject, but because it has been helpful to some women, I decided it might be worth mentioning.

From a readers' survey on the use of vitamin E, author Richard A. Passwater talks about vitamin E and its beneficial use in relieving menopausal symptoms. "Actually," writes Passwater, "there was no mention of menopause on the questionnaire. Yet, two thousand women volunteered that they found vitamin E to totally relieve the problems of menopause." Women claimed they had more energy and a sense of well-being, relief of leg cramps and hot flashes, as well as other menopausal problems.[2]

While this report may sound fantastic, vitamin E is not a proven therapy. Any and all plans to take vitamin-mineral supplements should be discussed with your doctor.

Exercise is especially important to us as we grow older. It improves circulation and, according to one of my sources, "Next to estrogen and calcium, weight bearing exercise [walking, jogging, bicycling, jumping rope] appears to be the most important technique for preserving bone. Exercise actually stimulates the formation of new bone in a woman's body."[3]

One special exercise I encourage you to do on a regular basis is Kegel's exercise. This exercise tightens up the muscles in the vaginal area. Relaxed, loose, or damaged muscle tissue can result in a prolapsed uterus. Kegel's not only helps prevent this problem, but also works to minimize urine leakage.

To do Kegel's exercise, simply tighten up the muscle (like you would to stop the flow of urine) and hold it for about two seconds. It may help to think in terms of tightening or pulling in and holding the whole bottom.

Sound simple? There's a catch: Kegel's only works with repetition—about three hundred times a day. No one knows you're doing it, however, so you can pull in that bottom any place, any time. You may want to try doing it in groups of twenty-five to fifty at a time.

Help for Vaginal Dryness

Lack of estrogen can cause a drying out of vaginal tissues and skin. Feel free to use lotions and lubricants on skin surfaces as needed. Also, you may want to keep some Vaseline or K-Y Jelly handy to prevent painful intercourse.

Vaginal dryness may not be relieved entirely by the estrogen tablets. If not, an estrogen cream is available for local application. You may want to ask your doctor about it if painful intercourse, vaginal dryness, and itching are a problem for you.

Estrogen Replacement Therapy

The most common treatment for women suffering symptoms resulting from a depleted store of estrogen is estrogen replacement therapy (ERT).

The effect of estrogen therapy on a premenopausal woman can be quite dramatic. Within a week, one can see a diminishing of hot flashes and many other symptoms. Often doctors will start with a low dosage and increase it if symptoms are not relieved.

Over the years doctors are seeing more and more benefits to keeping pre- and postmenopausal women on estrogen replacement therapy. According to a study published in the March 1, 1979, issue of the *American Journal of Obstetrics/Gynecology,* women treated with estrogen had "significantly lower rates of development of cardiovascular disease, hypertension, osteoporosis and fractures." Women on estrogen replacement therapy also needed fewer sedatives and tranquilizers. The women treated generally had fewer problems with weight gain, strokes, clogged arteries, and congestive heart failure.

There have been noted psychological benefits, as well. In the book *The Medical Management of Menopause and Premenopause,* I read that "Behavior and emotional scales indicated that women who took hormones became less neurotic with passage of time, more extroverted, less depressed, and that their concentration improved. Estrogen was noted to have a positive effect in improving libido, sexual activity, satisfaction, fantasy, and capacity for orgasm."[4]

When Do We Start ERT?

Perhaps the biggest question is not whether or not a woman should take estrogen, but when.

Doctors I've talked with about the matter don't consider it wise to wait until a woman's menstruation has ended to start estrogen replacement therapy. While caution is usually foremost on their minds, doctors will often begin treating women with the clinical symptoms of estrogen deficiency immediately—especially those who have a sudden loss of ovary function because of surgical menopause or radiation.

If estrogen hasn't been taken before menopause, it definitely should be started after. Dr. Sheldon Spielman, a noted gynecologist, expressed these concerns. "In order to prevent osteoporosis, estrogen must be given within a couple of years of the onset of menopause and maintained for life. If a woman waits too long to take estrogen, the bones will go through an irreversible change and the calcium loss will continue in spite of estrogen therapy."[5]

Estrogen and You

There are some things you should know about estrogen before you take it. Ask your doctor for specifics. Your questions may go something like this:

• Is the estrogen you're prescribing for me natural or synthetic?
• Will I be getting progesterone with it?
• What is the dosage?
• Will I be getting injections or pills?
• What side effects should I look for?
• What guidelines shall I use for adjusting the dose to meet my individual needs? (Some doctors will ask you to call them if you are having trouble, rather than make your own adjustments.)

Again, don't be afraid to find out exactly what you are getting and why. It's your body, and you have a right to know the details about the way it's treated.

In his book *1250 Health Care Questions Women Ask*, Dr. Joe

McIlhaney suggests a schedule of: "one 0.625 mg. tablet of conjugated estrogen or 0.05 mg. of ethinyl estradiol from the first day of the calendar month until the 25th day. With the last fourteen estrogen tablets you should also take a daily progesterone pill, such as 10 mg. Provera."

"If this dose of estrogen is not enough to prevent the symptoms of menopause, you can increase it so that you are taking two, three, or even four times as much estrogen as the 0.625 mg. that you started on," Dr. McIlhaney says, "but the 0.625 mg.-a-day dose is enough to maintain healthy bones."

Even though high dosages of estrogen can be taken, doctors suggest you try to keep the dose as low as possible, though not less than 0.625 mg. a day.[6]

Is It Really Menopause?

If the doctor is doubtful about whether or not you are premenopausal, he may want to take a cervical smear called the Karyopicnotic Index (K.I.), which can help determine the level of estrogen.

Many times doctors who suspect a woman is premenopausal but are unsure will prescribe a trial dose of estrogen for several months, to see if her symptoms are relieved.

Sometimes determining what is actually happening and whether or not your problems are related to hormones may take time. The best doctors, even those who routinely treat their patients with hormone therapy when necessary, are very careful about making the right diagnosis. They will want to check out all the body's systems, to make certain everything is in order. Side effects of estrogen therapy may include: nausea, bloating, headaches, and depression. These, however, generally only occur in women who have no estrogen deficiency (such as women with PMS). Other side effects may include vaginal bleeding.

Many women and their doctors have been extremely worried over another possible side effect of taking estrogen: the risk of cancer.

Estrogen and Cancer

Research over the past few years has helped to greatly reduce the risk of endometrial cancer in women on estrogen therapy.

The original estrogens, including Stilbestral, Dioenestral, and Hexoestradiol, were nonsteroidals that have been shown to be possible cancer-producing agents. They are very different from those naturally found in the body, and are rarely used today. Today the main source of estrogen is natural, taken from the urine of pregnant mares.

According to the American Medical Association's Council on Scientific Affairs, research has shown that "cyclic use of estrogen is apparently less hazardous than continuous administration."[7] *Cyclic* meaning that the estrogen is stopped for several days each month.

To further lower the risk of uterine and cervical cancer with estrogen replacement therapy, Dr. Penny Wise Budoff writes, "If you decide to take estrogen, insist upon the addition of progesterone."[8]

Her theory is based on the fact that women lose both estrogen and progesterone, thus both should be replaced. Progesterone given in sufficient quantities "counteracts, supercedes, and modifies the estrogen effect even when estrogen is given on a daily basis."[9]

Dr. Budoff concludes that "estrogen-progesterone therapy may help prevent osteoporosis, vaginal atrophy and infection, bladder changes, coronary heart disease, hot flashes, and emotional disturbances. As for risks," she says, "I have far less fear of uterine cancer than I have of broken bones and coronary artery disease. Uterine cancer is not as lethal."[10] By that comment, I would suspect she means uterine cancer can be detected early and usually eliminated surgically.

Dr. Budoff is not alone in her thinking. Dr. Joe Fraumeni, of the United States National Cancer Institute and one of the world's leading cancer experts, was quoted by Dr. Michael O'Donnell in an article, "New Light on the Mid-Life Crisis," as saying, "I would be concerned only by the promiscuous use of estrogens such as occurs in certain parts of the United States where estrogens are used almost as a 'youth drug' and women receive them whether they have symptoms or not."

An article in the January, 1983 issue of *JAMA*, titled "Estrogen Replacement in the Menopause" also indicated that "Women treated with estrogen-progestin combination have a lower incidence of endometrial cancer than women treated with estrogen alone."[11]

And Dr. Jean Hailes, director of the Melbourne Menopause Clinic, quoted by Dr. O'Donnell, concurs. "Small doses of the new safer estrogens in combination with other hormones, progestogens, have the great advantage of eliminating the risk of estrogens causing cancer of the womb. . . ."

The incidence of breast cancer in women who use estrogen has been a major concern in recent years. But the latest studies indicate that women taking estrogen plus progesterone during the postmenopausal years have a decreased chance of developing breast cancer.[12]

A very recent article in a local paper reported that contraceptives were no longer thought to cause breast cancer. A study done on over 9,000 women who had taken contraceptives for fifteen years or longer showed no increase in breast cancer due to taking the pill. However, experts still caution us in the use of hormones, as we have yet to see the lifelong effect of the drugs.

Beware the Risks

While this may sound all well and good, hormones are not the wonder drug of the century. There are drawbacks. Since estrogen/progesterone therapy is designed to follow a somewhat normal cycle, there may be withdrawal bleeding, a menses-like bleeding during the five days estrogen is not taken.

It is important that before you begin estrogen therapy you be aware of the risks and the benefits and that you and your doctor weigh them out carefully, based on your individual needs and your health. I would encourage you to learn all you can about menopause and current treatments.

Don't believe something just because your neighbor says so, and don't blindly accept everything your doctor tells you. Doctors are human, capable of human error. They often differ in their beliefs of how, when, and even if menopausal women should be treated. Some doctors wouldn't dare "interfere with mother nature," while others tend to hand out estrogen as if it were candy on Valentine's Day.

When Your Doctor Says No to ERT

There are times when estrogen therapy should be avoided. When your doctor says no to estrogen therapy, it may not be because he is out of tune with the times or not sensitive to your needs. It may well be because you have a history or health problem that flashes a warning signal to him. A doctor who generously hands out estrogen to his female patients without considering the risks is every bit as wrong as the one who pats you on the head and says, "My dear girl, women have been going through menopause since the beginning of time. You'll just have to live with it."

Before your doctor offers you estrogen replacement, he should do a complete physical and check your medical history to determine whether or not you are qualified to take it.

Here is a list of conditions where ERT is definitely contraindicated.

- Undiagnosed vaginal bleeding
- Cancer of the breast, uterus, or ovaries
- Pregnancy
- Past history of blood clots (thrombophlebitis)

There are also several conditions that pose potential problems for patients receiving estrogen. If you have any of these conditions, it doesn't mean you can't or shouldn't have estrogen. But you are at high risk for complications, and will need to be closely monitored. You should have a doctor's exam on a quarterly basis at the least, and more often if your doctor recommends it.

- Past history of coronary thrombosis
- Diabetes
- High blood pressure
- Liver disease
- Epilepsy or other seizure disorders
- Fibrocystic disease of the breast
- Connective tissue disease
- Family history of high cholesterol
- Gall bladder disease
- Multiple sclerosis
- Migraine headaches

Precautions are not just for people in a potential high-risk category. Anyone on estrogen therapy should have a checkup every six months: blood-pressure check, weight check, general exam, and Pap smear.

Estrogen therapy isn't the only treatment available for managing menopause. The earlier suggestions on diet, exercise, stress reduction, and attitudes work very well, no matter what phase of life you are in.

Even though individual doctors may disagree, the AMA's Council on Scientific Affairs has given the following recommendations regarding management of menopause. These principles may be helpful to you in knowing what you can and should expect from your doctor:

1. As with any form of drug therapy, estrogens should be used only for responsive indications, in the smallest effective dose, and for the shortest period that satisfies therapeutic need.

2. Estrogens are effective in the treatment or prevention of vasomotor flushes, atrophic urogenital conditions, and osteoporosis. Recent evidence also supports a protective effect against certain manifestations of arteriosclerotic heart disease.

3. When estrogen is given to menopausal women with intact uteri, cyclic administration is recommended to avoid continuous stimulation of the endometrium. A progestin may be added on the last seven to ten days of each estrogen cycle.

4. Topical estrogen preparations are useful in the treatment of vulvo-vaginal atrophic systems, but their ready absorption through the intact but atrophic epithelial surface requires that cumulative dosage be considered.

5. Any vaginal bleeding in the postmenopausal patient must be investigated promptly.

6. At least yearly monitoring of asymptomatic patients treated with estrogen should be performed and may include histological or cytological sampling. Pelvic and breast examinations and the measurement of BP should also be done.

7. Estrogen replacement therapy is specifically contraindicated in those patients with an estrogen-dependent neoplasm of the breast or a history of such a lesion.

8. As in all therapeutic decisions the patient should be fully informed of the relative risks and benefits before treatment is initiated, and the question of continued need should be reviewed periodically.[13]

Don't we live in a wonderful world? We no longer have to put up with hot flashes, painful intercourse, or any of the other symptoms that make life miserable for the menopausal woman. Not that all our troubles are over, but at least they are made easier to bear. We can have better health, both mentally and physically, as we move into the best phase of all: postmenopause.

Part V

Postmenopause ——— 🦢

Sometimes people think of the postmenopause as the end of life. But as we approach the final phase, it is anything but that. True, the reproductive system has closed down, but the postmenopausal woman is very much alive.

In this final chapter, we'll be talking about the realities of the postmenopause and giving you encouragement on making the final phase of your life the best.

16

The Last for
Which the First
Was Made   ৡ

In 1952, my husband and I and our three children moved to the United States, into full-time missionary service. Being born and raised in the very hot climate of south Australia, I found the Pacific Northwest extremely cold and uncomfortably wet.

To be honest, I have never been able to get used to the cold. Sometimes I long for my Australian homeland and the lovely warm climate. But I've adjusted. I make the best of it because, after all, what else can one do?

The postmenopause is like moving into a foreign place where there is definitely a change in climate. We might long for the early phases of our lives, which we remember as safe and secure—and young. But time doesn't allow us to linger, any more than it allows weather to remain the same.

I had to do a lot of adjusting when I moved to the United States. And as we move from middle age into maturity, we find ourselves coming through yet another period of adjustment.

Perhaps the most difficult part about postmenopause is the age. Most of us don't really mind leaving our childbearing years, or the organs that go with them, behind. It's the fear we don't like: fear of poor health, of being alone, of no longer being needed, of dying.

Life After Menopause

Postmenopause is the period of life after menopause. The reproductive system has ceased to function. The vagina has shrunk to near prepuberty size, and the ovaries, while they may continue to produce small amounts of estrogen, no longer provide follicles for fertilization. But today all this doesn't mean the end.

One of the greatest myths ever to be embraced by our society is that when a woman reaches menopause she reaches the end of life. Actually, before the advent of modern medicine and estrogen replacement therapy, the myth wasn't too far from wrong. A woman's health often deteriorated rather quickly after menopause. Lack of estrogen not only left women with withered reproductive organs, but withered bodies, as well.

Life expectancy for women in the fourteenth century was about 33 years. By the early 1900s the average life expectancy for women had risen to 48 years. Then, most women never lived long enough to be postmenopausal. Today, however, because the average woman's life expectancy is between 70 and 80 years, menopause is at the midpoint in our lives. It is a point where we can rise out of the cocoon of the first half of our menarcheal lives and fly as uninhibited as a butterfly through the second.

New Energy

The postmenopause is what psychoanalyst Therese Benedek, M.D., called a developmental phase.[1] Notice she did not say "declining," or "disintegrating," but *developmental*. Of course it is not biologically developmental, because aging does occur, and our bodies will eventually die. Sometimes physical problems can be a detrimental factor in what we accomplish in our older years. But for most of us, this developmental phase means it's time to let go and grow.

For years we women have expended vast resources of energy toward the menstrual cycle and menopause, our children, our husbands, and jobs. Now that menstruation is over and the reproductive system has closed down, our bodies are free to redirect that energy.

Here are some things we can expect to happen during this liberating phase of our lives.

- There is a rising tide of energy levels.
- Our general health is better. We're rejuvenated.
- We have increased sexual enjoyment. No more worries about getting pregnant. Our "sex lives often become more spontaneous and satisfying. Although there is no longer the fiery passion of youth, sex becomes expressive of a tried and trusted companionship and intimacy often more satisfactory in its total meaning than earlier experiences."[2]
- We have more independence.
- We have a new desire or drive for learning and socialization.
- We have greater capacity to think, learn, grow, and master new things.
- We have freedom to give of ourselves in service.
- We have greater capacity to love more widely and unconditionally.
- There are often new areas of self-gratification—a release of skills, qualities, and talents never before experienced.[3]
- Women in postmenopause gain new self-confidence.

Unfortunately, our society has little or no respect for old age or wisdom. I encourage you not to be caught up in the directives of our youth-oriented culture. They say you are past your prime after forty. They say your worth diminishes with age. They say it's time to retire. I say *nonsense*. Look, I've been postmenopausal for twenty years, and I have yet to achieve my full potential. I don't think I've ever had so much energy and zest for life. I echo the sentiments of poet Robert Browning:

> Grow old along with me,
> The best is yet to be,
> The last of life, for which the first was made.
> Our times are in His hand
> Who saith, "A whole I planned,
> Youth shows but half;
> Trust God: see all, nor be afraid!"

I can personally attest to life after menopause. I have an insatiable appetite for learning. I'm enjoying recognition among my peers that I've never had before. Postmenopause has brought me a sort of peace, and I like it.

Besides myself, there are plenty of other women who perhaps did or are doing their best work in their postmenopausal years.

Aging, Yet Ageless

Golda Meir was a great example of an ageless woman. The late prime minister of Israel had tremendous drive and ambition. She governed Israel from the ages of seventy-one to seventy-six. Late in life, when she transitioned into postmenopause, her family urged her to slow down and not work so hard. "Why?" she asked. "I have more energy and better health now than since I was a young girl!"

Other examples of ageless wonders include: Katharine Hepburn, who is still a leading lady; best-selling authors like the late Helen Steiner Rice, Corrie ten Boom, and Catherine Marshall. Women in postmenopause often hold high government positions: Indira Gandhi, Margaret Thatcher, Queen Elizabeth, and of course, the gracious Queen Mother.

I encourage you to look at postmenopause as a challenge. Here are a few ideas that might start you on your way.

Get involved   You'll want to do something with this new flush of energy. I would suggest for starters that you develop a hobby or get involved in a social group or community project. The important thing is to get and keep busy.

Be encouraged by others   Read books and stories about others who are not only surviving but thriving in their final but glorious phase. Also try reading self-help books that are designed to encourage you and lift your spirits.

Recommit your life to a higher goal   Recommit yourself on a daily basis to being the best you can be. Commit your life daily to living victoriously for the God who is your source of life. I know many women who have experienced miraculous physical healing during their life's journey. God—the Holy Spirit, Counselor, Comforter—provides the power and strength to help us face each new day.

God has been with me through each phase of my life. I'm not sure I could have made it without Him. I have been through a lot of hard times, both physically and mentally, but through it all, God's grace has been and still is sufficient for me.

My desire is that each of you will grow and develop through each phase of your life with the knowledge that the turbulence associated with the phases will eventually end.

The Emotional Phases of Your Life

For centuries women have been going through emotional ups and downs brought about by the hormonal changes going on in their bodies. And for centuries we've been misunderstood, misinformed, and mistreated. More and more health-care professionals are recognizing the special needs—mental, emotional, and physical—of women during their reproductive years and beyond.

We're making progress, and I thank God for that. But now it's time for you to take what you've learned and pass it on.

• Help yourself. Learn all you can about your particular problem area and take advantage of the resources available to you.

• Help your friends. Talk about experiences, learn together, and support one another in prayer, understanding, compassion, and love.

• Help your community. Form support groups for women who need the encouragement this book can bring. In my introduction, I said my desire in writing *Emotional Phases of a Woman's Life* was to "shed a clearer light to brighten your path. . . ." If I have succeeded in brightening your darkness, please share that light with others.

With enough knowledge, with enough prayer, with enough light, we just might end the darkness.

Appendix

List of premenstrual feelings, attitudes, and behavior changes, as reported to me in over thirty years of practice and research.

unspiritual feelings	impaired self-control
lack of concentration	impaired judgment
tremors	impaired willpower
needs extra sleep	hazy thinking
depressed, tiredness	expressed resentment
nervous tension	rattled
savage	hypercritical
weepy	biting in speech
temper outbursts	suspicious
loss of self-control	distrustful
frustration	apprehension
fear of losing control	forgetfulness
outbursts of emotion	fatigue
jumpiness	moody
abnormal excitement	talking too much
hair-trigger temperament	sense of loss
catatonic depression	melancholia

thoughtless
absentminded
supersensitive
irrational
shouts
no insights
impulsive
negative attitudes to self
split personality
food binges
crave salty/spicy foods
ravenous hunger
compulsive eating
irritated when hungry
feeling of forever
spending sprees
striking or spectacular
   change of behavior
irritable
shaky
jitters
sluggish
witchy; bitchy
sudden mood swings
uptight—can't relax
loss of security
agitation
restless energy
abnormal emotions
high-strung temperament
manic activity
recurrent frenzy

hyper manic trends
forboding sensations of im-
   pending insecurity
cyclic alteration of personality 10 days prior
expressed hostility
captious
short-tempered
lash out for no reason
jealous
low self-esteem
anxiety
fretfulness
lethargic
crying over anything
blanket-of-fog feeling
desire to be alone
careless
unpunctual
morbid memories
horrid
hateful
fights
makes mistakes—has acci-
   dents
self-depreciation
negative attitude to others
abnormally hungry
tolerance for sugar
cravings for food
touch-me-not attitude
change in sexual behavior

Source Notes 　 ɞ

Introduction
1. Niels H. Lauersen and Eileen Stukane, *Premenstrual Syndrome and You* (New York: Simon & Schuster, 1983), cover.

Chapter 3
1. Penny Wise Budoff, M.D., *No More Menstrual Cramps and Other Good News* (New York: G. P. Putnam's Sons, 1980), p. 40.

Chapter 4
1. Joe S. McIlhaney, Jr., M.D., and Susan Nethery, *1250 Health-Care Questions Women Ask* (Grand Rapids, Mich.: Baker Book House, 1985), pp. 445–46.
See also "Painful Periods (Dysmenorrhea)," flyer PR-06-R-0457-P-2A (Morris Plains, N.J.: Parke-Davis, 1982). "Primary Menstrual Dysfunction," flyer PD-06-FD-1274-P-1 (Morris Plains, N.J.: Parke-Davis, 1983).

Chapter 5
1. Joe S. McIlhaney, Jr., M.D., with Susan Nethery. *1250 Health-Care Questions Women Ask* (Grand Rapids, Mich.: Baker Book House, 1985), pp. 445–46.
2. Ibid.

Chapter 8

1. James C. Dobson, "Focus on the Family," tape CS166.
2. Gillian Ford, *Premenstrual Syndrome Relief* (Newcastle, Calif.: PMS Relief).
3. Katharina Dalton, *Once a Month* (Claremont, Calif.: Hunter House, 1983), pp. 50–59.
4. Ibid.
5. Carol Havens, "Premenstrual Syndrome," *Postgraduate Medicine* 177:7 (May 15, 1985): 32.
6. Dalton, *Once a Month*, p. xv.
7. Coleen B. Demarest, ed., "PMS: Is It Just a Fad Diagnosis?" *Patient Care* (April 30, 1985): 68.
See also J. T. Hargrove and G. E. Abraham, "The Incidence of Premenstrual Tension in a Gynecological Clinic," *The Journal of Reproductive Medicine* 27 (1982): 721–24.
8. Penny Wise Budoff, M.D., *No More Menstrual Cramps and Other Good News* (New York: G. P. Putnam's Sons, 1980).
9. Dalton, *Once a Month*, pp. 147–48.
10. Budoff, *No More Menstrual Cramps*, p. 239.

Chapter 9

1. Douglas W. Laube, M.D., "Premenstrual Syndrome," *The Female Patient*, vol. 10 (June 1985): 61.
2. Michelle Harrison, *Self-Help for Premenstrual Syndrome* (Cambridge, Mass.: Matrix Press, 1982, 1984), pp. 28–29.
3. Ibid., p. 34.
4. Ibid.
5. Ibid.
6. Ibid., p. 40.
7. Carol Havens, "Premenstrual Syndrome," *Postgraduate Medicine* 177:7 (May 15, 1985): 36.

Chapter 11

1. G. Virginia Upton, "The Perimenopause: Physiologic Correlates and Clinical Management," *The Journal of Reproductive Medicine* 27:1 (January, 1982).

2. Ibid.

3. Niels H. Lauersen and Eileen Stukane, *Premenstrual Syndrome and You* (New York: Simon & Schuster, 1983), p. 1.

Chapter 12

1. G. Virginia Upton, "The Perimenopause: Physiologic Correlates and Clinical Management," *The Journal of Reproductive Medicine* 27:1 (January, 1982): 11–12.

Chapter 14

1. James C. Dobson, *Dr. Dobson Answers Your Questions* (Wheaton, Ill.: Tyndale, 1982), p. 394.

2. Joe S. McIlhaney, Jr., M.D., with Susan Nethery, *1250 Health-Care Questions Women Ask* (Grand Rapids, Mich.: Baker Book House, 1985), p. 17.

3. Ibid., 176.

4. Katharina Dalton, *Once a Month* (Claremont, Calif.: Hunter House, 1983), p. 154.

5. Ibid.

6. Ibid., p. 155.

7. Penny Wise Budoff, M.D., *No More Menstrual Cramps and Other Good News* (New York: G. P. Putnam's Sons, 1980), p. 193.

Chapter 15

1. Joe S. McIlhaney, Jr., M.D., with Susan Nethery, *1250 Health-Care Questions Women Ask* (Grand Rapids, Mich.: Baker Book House, 1985), p. 183.

2. Richard Passwater, "Vitamin E and Menopause," *Prevention* (July, 1976): 91.

3. McIlhaney and Nethery, *1250 Questions*, p. 183.

4. Cutler and Garcia, *The Medical Management of Menopause and Premenopause* (Philadelphia: J. B. Lippincott, 1984), p. 39.

5. Ruby MacDonald, *Forty Plus and Feeling Fabulous* (Old Tappan, N. J.: Fleming H. Revell Co., 1982), p. 81.

6. McIlhaney and Nethery, *1250 Questions*, pp. 184–85.

7. The Council on Scientific Affairs, "Estrogen Replace-

ment in the Menopause," *The Journal of the American Medical Association* 249: 3 (January 21, 1983): 360.

8. Penny Wise Budoff, M.D., *No More Menstrual Cramps and Other Good News* (New York: G. P. Putnam's Sons, 1980), p. 215.

9. Ibid., p. 200.

10. Ibid., p. 215.

11. Council on Scientific Affairs, "Estrogen Replacement," p. 360.

12. McIlhaney and Nethery, *1250 Questions*, p. 186.

13. Council on Scientific Affairs, "Estrogen Replacement," p. 361.

Chapter 16

1. Therese Benedek, *Studies in Psychosomatic Medicine* (New York: The Ronald Press), 1952, p. 352.

2. Clara Thompson, *On Women* (New York: New American Library, 1971), p. 171.

3. Benedek, *Psychosomatic Medicine*, pp. 352–72.

Suggested Reading   ~

Books

Budoff, Penny Wise, M.D. *No More Menstrual Cramps and Other Good News*. New York: G.P. Putnam's Sons, 1980.

Dalton, Katharina, M.D. *Once a Month*. Claremont, Calif.: Hunter House, 1983.

Dobson, James C., Dr. *Dobson Answers Your Questions*. Wheaton, Ill.: Tyndale, 1982.

Harrison, Michelle, M.D. *Self-Help for Premenstrual Syndrome*. Cambridge, Mass.: Matrix Press, 1982, 1984.

Lauersen, Niels H., and Eileen Stukane. *Premenstrual Syndrome and You*. New York: Simon & Schuster, 1983.

McIlhaney, Joe S., Jr., M.D. with Susan Nethery. *1250 Health-Care Questions Women Ask*. Grand Rapids, Mich.: Baker Book House, 1985.

Weideger, Paula. *Menstruation and Menopause, the Physiology and Psychology, the Myth and Reality*. New York: Knopf, 1976.

Newsletters and Support Organizations

PMS ACCESS Newsletter, PMS Access, PO Box 9326, Madison, WI 53715, Phone 1-800-222-4PMS. Gives access to books, educational opportunities and materials, counseling and treatment programs, and workshops and seminars.

PMS Relief, PO Box 10, Newcastle, CA 95658, Phone (916) 888-7677. Provides information, educational opportunities, and counseling.

For Your Doctor: All material as listed above plus . . .

Books

Chihal, Dr. H. Jane, M.D., Ph.D. *Premenstrual Syndrome—A Clinic Manual.* Durant, Okla.: Creative Infomatics, 1985.

Dalton, Katharina, M.D. *The Premenstrual Syndrome and Progesterone Therapy.* Chicago: Year Book Medical Publishers, 1977.

Other

PMS: NEWS & VIEWS, a Chattem Bulletin for Physicians and other health professionals, is published by CHATTEM Professional Services, 1715 West 38th St., Chattanooga, TN 37409.

Kline, Monte, PhD. "Natural Answers to PMS," in *Christian Health Counselor,* Total Living, PO Box 780, Eagle Point, OR 97524, December 1985, Issue 07.

"Sexual Medicine Today," A Supplement to *Medical Tribune,* June 16, 1982, pp. 4–11.

Upton, G. Virginia, Ph.D. "The Perimenopause: Physiologic Correlates and Clinical Management," *The Journal of Reproductive Medicine* 27:1, January 1982.